Using Action Research to Improve Instruction

Action research is increasingly used as a means for teachers to improve their instruction, yet for many teachers the idea of doing "research" can be somewhat intimidating. *Using Action Research to Improve Instruction* offers a comprehensive, easy-to-understand approach to action research in classroom settings. This engaging and accessible guide is grounded in sources of data readily available to teachers, such as classroom observations, student writing, surveys, interviews, and tests. Organized to mirror the action research process, the highly interactive format prompts readers to discover a focus, create research questions, address design and methodology, collect information, conduct data analysis, communicate the results, and to generate evidence-based teaching strategies. Engaging in these decision-making processes builds the skills essential to action research and promotes a deeper understanding of teaching practice.

Special features include:

■ an interactive text
■ reflection questions and activity prompts
■ a sample action research report
■ numerous examples and practice examples
■ numbered sections for cross referencing.

This original text is a must-read for teachers interested in how they can use their current knowledge of instruction and assessment to meaningfully engage in action research.

John E. Henning is Associate Professor of Educational Psychology at the University of Northern Iowa. He is also author of *The Art of Discussion-based Teaching* (Routledge, 2007).

Jody M. Stone is Professor of Education at the University of Northern Iowa.

James L. Kelly is Professor in the Department of Teaching at the University of Northern Iowa.

Using Action Research to Improve Instruction

An Interactive Guide for Teachers

JOHN E. HENNING, JODY M. STONE, AND JAMES L. KELLY

Routledge
Taylor & Francis Group

NEW YORK AND LONDON

First published 2009
by Routledge
270 Madison Ave, New York, NY 10016

Simultaneously published in the UK
by Routledge
2 Park Square, Milton Park, Abingdon, Oxon OX14 4RN

Routledge is an imprint of the Taylor & Francis Group, an informa business

© 2009 Taylor & Francis

Typeset in Minion Pro by
Book Now Ltd, London
Printed and bound in the United States of America
on acid-free paper by Edwards Brothers, Inc.

Library of Congress Cataloging-in-Publication Data
Henning, John E.
Using action research to improve instruction: an interactive guide for teachers / John E.
Henning, Jody M. Stone, and James L. Kelly.
     p. cm.
Includes bibliographical references and index.
1. Action research in education. 2. Effective teaching. 3. Teachers—In-service training.
I. Stone, Jody M. II. Kelly, James L., 1942– III. Title.
LB1028.24.H466 2009
370.72—dc22   2008021834

ISBN-10: 0–415–99173–0 (hbk)
ISBN-10: 0–415–99174–9 (pbk)
ISBN-10: 0–203–88729–8 (ebk)

ISBN-13: 978–0–415–99173–5 (hbk)
ISBN-13: 978–0–415–99174–2 (pbk)
ISBN-13: 978–0–203–88729–5 (ebk)

December 12, 2008

Contents

List of Figures

List of Tables

Preface

The primary aim of this book is to provide a comprehensive and easy-to-understand introduction to using action research in school settings. It is written for teachers who are interested in: (1) improving their teaching practice through systematic self-analysis; (2) taking an active role in their school's continuous improvement process; and (3) collecting evidence that demonstrates their skill as a teacher.

For many teachers, the idea of doing "research" can be somewhat intimidating. This book is designed to show teachers how they can use their current knowledge of instruction and assessment to engage in action research. Thus, many of the action research methods discussed in this book deal with data sources that are already familiar to teachers, such as observing students, assessing writing, comparing pre and post tests, and using other forms of classroom assessment. However, this is not intended to be a book about classroom assessment. Therefore, there is little discussion of test or rubric construction. Instead the focus is on how to plan, collect, analyze, and reflect on data for the purpose of evaluating or developing new teaching strategies.

Learning these skills entails more than simply reading about them. Thus, this book is organized in an interactive format. As you work through the book, you will be prompted to create research questions, to decide on your research participants, to interpret action research data, and to use the results of your analysis to design new teaching strategies. You will benefit from this process to the degree you are able to respond completely and thoughtfully to the questions that are posed. By fully participating, you will become more skilled at:

- observing students;
- analyzing existing school and classroom data;
- making inferences based on school data;
- using data to develop new teaching strategies;
- working collaboratively in teacher study groups.

This book aims to be comprehensive in its treatment of school-related action research data, including data from observations of students and their work, observations of teaching, survey and interview data, standardized achievement test, and pre and post tests. Because there is variation in the way these forms of data are collected and analyzed, each is presented in a separate chapter. This approach enables us to present a more specific and detailed view of each action research method. Using this approach will help you apply what you read to your own action research projects more easily and quickly.

The book is organized into five parts. Part I consists of two chapters that introduce action research: Chapter 1 defines and describes action research and Chapter 2 shows you how to plan an action research project. The final part (Part V) consists of two chapters on how to talk and write about action research data. Parts II–IV consist of six chapters organized into three pairs according to the type of data discussed: observational data, survey or interview data, and test data. In each of these chapters, you will learn techniques specific to a particular form of data. At the beginning of each chapter, each approach to action research will be defined, illustrated with examples, and compared to other types of action research based on its relative benefits and limitations. As you move through each chapter, you will be engaged in creating a research question, deciding on your participants, designing data collection methods, analyzing data, and developing new teaching strategies.

In Part II, Chapters 3 and 4 will show you how to observe students and teachers in classroom settings. Examples include observing students while they are working, making observations of student work, and observing teacher interactions with students. This form of analysis lacks the objectivity of test data, but it is much more useful for specifically diagnosing learning problems and generating new strategies to address them.

In Part III, Chapters 5 and 6 address the use of surveys and interviews to investigate the perceptions of students, parents, teachers, and administrators. These two sources of data can provide insight into your respondents' thinking, such as students' perceptions of your teaching methods, parents' perceptions of school climate, and teachers' perceptions of school programs. Both surveys and interviews can serve as a helpful complement to other sources of data.

In Part IV, Chapters 7 and 8 address the use of standardized achievement tests and pre and post testing data. Both of these approaches are helpful when trying to assess either the progress of a single class or an entire school. They can provide objective evidence of whether your strategies are working, help you identify strengths and weaknesses in the curriculum, illustrate the progress of specific subgroups of students, and identify the strengths and weaknesses of individual students.

In Part V, Chapters 9 and 10 will show teachers how to collaborate on data analysis and communicate their findings to others. Chapter 9 will address how to organize and structure a data assessment team. Chapter 10 will show teachers how to write an action research report. If you are planning to collaborate with other teachers or disseminate your findings to other teachers, parents or administrators; you may want to read these chapters sooner rather than later. For example, after reading the chapter on standardized achievement tests, you may want to read Chapter 10 to find out how to write an action research report on standardized achievement test data.

After you have finished this interactive guide, you will be able to do all of the following for each of the approaches to action research described in this book:

- Identify an area of concern that is related to instruction.
- Formulate a research question for investigating the identified area of concern.
- Search the existing educational literature.
- Collect data, evidence, or information that is involved with the research question.
- Make observations about the data you have collected.
- Interpret your data.
- Develop new teaching strategies.
- Justify the teaching strategies you have developed.
- Write up your findings into a coherent report.

Format of the Book

This book is organized in an interactive format based on the premise that learning how to do action research requires more than simply reading. Like teaching, conducting action research cannot be completely understood without engaging in the process. Thus, the questions posed in this text are more than simply review questions. Often new ideas are presented through the interactive format. In addition, many of the exercises are intended to familiarize you with the thinking processes associated with action research. For example, Chapters 3–8 have been designed so that upon their successful completion, you will be able to plan, conduct, and analyze an action research study using the method discussed in that chapter, e.g., observing students, observing teachers, administering surveys, conducting interviews, analyzing standardized tests, and comparing pre and post tests. By fully engaging in the interactive format, you will acquire fresh perspectives on action research that will deepen your understanding of the text and provide valuable experience in thinking like a researcher.

Acknowledgements

We would like to thank all the inservice and preservice teachers who provided feedback on the chapters in this book. We would also like to acknowledge that parts of Chapter 4, 7, and 9 are based on previous publications.

Chapter 4

Some information on observing teachers has previously been published in three previous works:

Henning, J.E. (2008). *The art of discussion-based teaching: Opening up conversation in the classroom.* New York: Routledge.

Henning, J.E. (2005). Leading discussions: Opening up the conversation. *College Teaching, 53* (3), 90–94.

Henning, J.E., & Lockhart, A. (2003) Acquiring the art of classroom discourse: A comparison of teacher and preservice teacher talk in a fifth grade classroom. *Research for Educational Reform, 8* (3), 46–57.

Chapter 7

Parts of the chapter on standardized testing were based on:

Henning, J.E. (2006). Teacher leaders at work: Analyzing standardized achievement data to improve instruction. *Education, 126* (4), 729–737.

Chapter 9

The information on teacher collaboration was based on work previously published in:

Henning, J.E. (2008). *The art of discussion-based teaching: Opening up conversation in the classroom.* New York: Routledge.

Part I
Introduction

Part I consists of a two-chapter introduction to action research. Chapter 1 defines action research and distinguishes it from other types of educational research. Key differences include the location of the research, the sources of data, the selection of participants, and the type of data analysis. In comparison to teaching, action research calls for more systematic, deliberate decision-making based on an explicit process. Chapter 2 will show you how to plan an action research project. Action research often begins when an episode arouses your curiosity, when you try to solve a difficult problem, or perhaps simply from a desire to get better. Ideas for action research projects can come from observations of your students, other teachers, professional development programs, or the educational literature. They can be further enhanced through a literature search that yields additional strategies and evidence concerning their effectiveness. Planning also requires a consideration of the methods you will use to collect data in your study. The thinking skills and dispositions described in the opening two chapters will be cultivated throughout this book by providing repeated practice in a four-step cycle of action research: plan, collect data, analyze, and reflect.

one
An Introduction to Action Research

I have lost much of the faith I once had in the consequences of asking only the professional educational researcher to study the schools and to recommend what they should do. Incorporating these recommendations into behavior patterns of practitioners involves some problems that so far have been insoluble … most of the study of what should go and what should be added must be done in thousands of classrooms and American communities. These studies must be undertaken by those who may have to change the way they do things as a result of the studies. Our schools cannot keep up with the life they are supposed to sustain and improve unless teachers, pupils, supervisors, administrators, and school patrons continuously examine what they are doing. Singly or in groups, they must use their imaginations creatively and constructively to identify the practices that must be changed to meet the needs and demands of modern life, courageously try out practices that give better promise and methodically and systemically gather evidence to test their work.

This is the process I call action research. I hold no special brief for the name, but it has some currency and is sufficiently descriptive. It is research that is undertaken by educational practitioners because they believe that by so doing they can make better decisions and engage in better actions.

(Stephen M. Corey, 1953, p. viii)

1 What is Educational Research?

The word "research" is used all the time. It appears in our newspapers. It can be heard spoken on the radio or by a television commentator during a news bulletin. As teachers or prospective teachers, you were or are very much aware from your undergraduate studies that educational research is an integral part of the education process. So when you hear this word used, you undoubtedly conjure up some vision of what this means to you. So what is educational research?

Reflection 1.1

In your own words, give a definition of education research. In a second paragraph, describe your perception of the value of research as it applies to education.

_____

_____

_____

Many people mistakenly believe that conducting research necessarily involves the use of statistics. This mistaken notion can prohibit the use of action research because teachers often find the idea of employing a complex statistical analysis intimidating, while others make the mistake of believing that research is not valid without a statistical analysis. In actuality, research and statistical analysis are not synonymous. There are quite a few ways to do educational research without using statistics. These approaches to research are not inferior to those requiring statistical analysis nor do they necessarily yield lesser or less certain information. So while statistical analysis is very useful and particularly helpful when dealing with large numbers of research participants or a large quantity of numerical data, it is important to recognize that there are many approaches to doing research, that each has its own particular strengths and limitations, and that each can make its own unique contribution to understanding whatever issue or problem is under study.

> Anyone who tries to get better evidence of the success or failure of his teaching or administrative or supervisory activities, and what he does in light of this evidence is conducting a type of action research.
> (Corey, 1949, p. 149)

Research methods that utilize statistical analysis and numerical data are classified as quantitative research. Approaches to research that do not involve a statistical analysis and a minimal use of numerical data are classified as qualitative research. In recent decades, qualitative research has gained increasing prominence in the field of educational research. A qualitative approach makes use of interviews, open-ended surveys, observations, and the analysis of teacher and student interactions. It is much more oriented to the use and interpretation of language rather than numbers. A vast number of qualitative studies have shown that qualitative research can enrich our understanding of teaching and learning.

Reflection 1.2 is a brief summary of the differences between quantitative and qualitative approaches to research.

So for those who are new to the research process and feel leery of research due to a dread of statistics, there is hope. First, you can feel reassured that doing research is more than simply using statistics. Second, this self-study guide deals exclusively with action research, which is primarily concerned with qualitative research. The analysis of numbers is minimal and simplified. The statistical concepts used in this book are already familiar to most educators, such as mean, median, and mode.

Reflection 1.2

Differences between quantitative and qualitative research

Quantitative research:

  is oriented towards numbers

  has large numbers of participants

  examines a quantity of data

  is interested in how much and how many relies on statistical analysis

  is interested in universal conclusions

  includes concepts such as random sampling, control groups, and statistical analyses

Qualitative research:

  is more oriented towards language

  has relatively few participants

  examines less data in more depth

  is concerned with specific qualities has analysis varied by context

  draws conclusions specific to a context

  is often based on individual case studies

Reflection 1.3

Identify each of the following research projects as either qualitative or quantitative:

_____ 1 Interview a group of principals about the effects of the No Child Left Behind legislation.

_____ 2 Determine the better of two instructional methods by comparing the average test score of two groups of students.

_____ 3 Observe school hallways between classes to determine the traffic patterns.

_____ 4 Survey students to determine their reading preferences.

_____ 5 Analyze trends for standardized achievement tests.

---

2 What is Action Research?

Author-educator Geoffrey Mills (2000) identifies action research as "Any systematic inquiry conducted by teacher researchers, principals, school counselors, or other stakeholders in the teaching/learning environment to gather information about how their particular schools operate, how they teach, and how well their students learn."

Can teachers do research? The answer to this question is a resounding, "You bet we can!" The very act of teaching involves collecting information to improve instruction. While some may not make a conscious effort to do research, all reflective teachers constantly plan new strategies, watch how students respond to them, and then think about how to make further improvements.

For example, here is a summary of how a teacher improved his approach to main-streaming (Fenstermacher, 1994):

> There are two essential aims of all action research: to *improve* and to *involve*. Action research aims at improvement in three areas: firstly, the improvement of a *practice;* secondly, the improvement of the *understanding* of the practice by its practitioners; and thirdly, the improvement of the *situation* in which the practice takes place. Those involved in the practice being considered are to be involved in the action research project in all its phases of planning, acting, observing, and reflecting. As an action research project develops, it is expected that a widening circle of those affected by the practice will become involved in the research process.
>
> (Carr & Kemmis, 1986, p. 165)

[The teacher] responds that he has worked very hard on this feature of his teaching; he states that he is a strong believer in the moral principles that sustain mainstreaming but really did not know how it would work in practice until he tried it. As this teacher continues to address my questions, he sets forth an account of what he does and why he does it. In other words, he provides reasons that make it clear that it was his desire and intention to work with the class in the manner that I observed and that his procedures for doing so are the result of many trial-and-error efforts, readings, talking with teachers, and talking with the students themselves about their perceptions of his teaching. In this example, the teacher is offering good reasons to explain his actions, reasons that, when taken together and arrayed in some coherent order, constitute a justification for the claim that this teacher knows how to promote student engagement in mainstreamed classrooms. (pp. 44–45)

This process of experimentation and reflection can be enhanced by action research, which is a type of research that can be used to great effect in school settings. Simply put, action research is undertaken for the purpose of improving student learning by introducing more effective teaching strategies. Action research has been shown to improve student achievement, provide opportunities for professional development, help teachers make their practice more explicit, and serve as a pre-professional activity for preservice teachers (Zeichner & Noffke, 2001).

The purpose of action research is to solve a problem here and now, in a local setting. In contrast, educational research addresses issues that can be applied in a wide variety of educational settings. This fundamental difference in how the two forms of research are conceived leads to other, more practical differences, such as who does the research, where and how it's done, how it is analyzed, and how it is utilized. For example, educational research may take place inside or outside of schools, while action research almost always takes place in a school setting. Studies in educational research require that researchers be very selective about choosing participants, while teachers are primarily interested in researching the students assigned to them. Educational researchers maintain careful control over what data is collected and when it is collected, while teachers must usually rely on data sources that are commonly available in schools. Educational researchers are more likely to have access to expertise in statistics or research from their colleagues: teachers must base their decisions on less technical analyses of the data.

Reflection 1.4

You have now read a number of definitions and have probably formed an impression of action research. So let's take a stab at creating your own definition. In the space below, write a working definition for action research. It may change somewhat as you continue with this course of study, but for now it has personal meaning to you.

_____

_____

_____

_____

---

3 Creating a Research Persona

To become effective action researchers, teachers need to take on a *research persona*. More precisely, this means to acquire a set of dispositions and behaviors that are associated with collecting and analyzing data. The research persona needed to conduct action research differs somewhat from a teaching persona. For example, when giving instruction, teachers usually address issues in the classroom in a very holistic way. In rapid succession or even simultaneously, teachers must handle issues related to classroom management, motivation, student learning, and assessment. These interactions with students require quick decisions with little opportunity to reflect or assess their effectiveness. Therefore, it matters very little to teachers how they arrive at solutions: what is important is that they find a solution that works—and fast.

In contrast, when teachers engage with action research, they need to examine problems more analytically. That means they must isolate specific elements of their teaching; then make specific, deliberate alterations in their instruction, collect data to evaluate their new strategy, and carefully analyze the data collected. These thinking processes require a different set of dispositions than the quick decisions made in a classroom while teaching. When engaged with students, teachers should be supportive,

The idea of the teacher as a researcher has a long history in education. The first well-known advocate of teacher research was Francis W. Parker, who promoted observational research to promote child-centered teaching methods in the later half of the nineteenth century (McFarland & Stansell, 1993). Action research began during the 1930s with the work of John Collier, a U.S. commissioner of Indian affairs and Kurt Lewin, a social psychologist. Stephen Corey is best known for his efforts to legitimatize action research in education, described in his book *Action Research to Improve School Practices* (Noffke, 1997). Beginning in the mid-1980s there has been a resurgent interest in action research under various names, such as teacher research, practitioner research, and self study.

encouraging, involved, empathetic, and extroverted. When engaged with data, teachers should be objective, detached, contemplative, and introverted. Acquiring the dispositions and thinking skills associated with action research is a significant part of cultivating a research persona.

Reflection 1.5

As a teacher who does action research, you must know when to call on your teaching persona and when to call on your research persona. For each of the teacher activities described below, distinguish between the two types of thinking described above. Identify the on-the-spot, intuitive, results-oriented, decision-making associated with teaching with a "T" and the more deliberate, more analytical, more systematic thinking associated with action research with an "R":

_____ 1 Examining student writing in a teacher study group.

_____ 2 Responding to student questions.

_____ 3 Interpreting standardized achievement test results.

_____ 4 Comparing pre- and post-tests.

_____ 5 Giving feedback as a student solves a problem.

_____ 6 Giving directions.

_____ 7 Interpreting the results of a survey.

---

4 Plan, Collect Data, Analyze, and Reflect

> Action research is simply a form of self-reflective inquiry undertaken by participants in social situations [teachers] in order to improve the rationality and justice of their own practices.
>
> (Carr and Kemmis, 1986, 162)

Action research can be described in four steps: *plan, collect data, analyze, and reflect* (Figure 1.1). Carefully thinking through each step of the process fosters a disposition for thoroughness, a heightened awareness of the thinking skills associated with action research, and an increased flexibility and control over your thought processes. Below, you will find an initial description of each of the four steps. These steps will serve as a basis for approaching each type of data collection described in the book.

1 *Plan*: Like teaching, planning is the first phase of the action research process. When planning a lesson, teachers establish learning goals, create an assessment plan, and design their instructional activities. When planning an action research study, teachers should decide on the goals and purposes of the study, decide on a research question to guide the study, select the research participants, and determine the method of data collection. Lacking a plan, you are likely to find yourself sifting aimlessly through piles of data without any clear purpose. Such an approach will most likely result in superficial findings. As you work through the book, you will be asked to develop plans for several different types of research. For some forms of data, it is helpful to know how the data is analyzed before try-

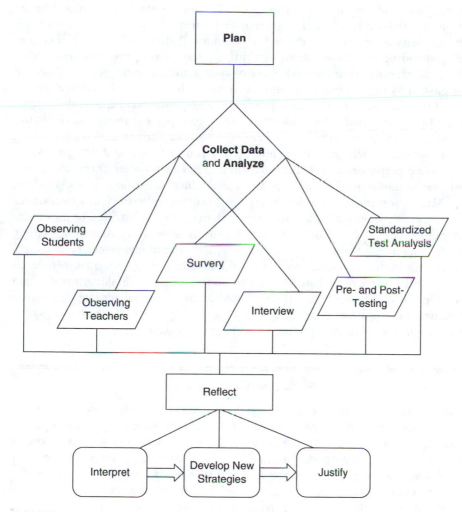

FIGURE 1.1 Plan, collect data, analyze, and reflect

ing to develop a plan. For these forms of data, the analysis will be presented before you are asked to create a plan.

2 **Collect data**: During the data collection phase, actions are taken to carry out your action research project. These actions include implementing new teaching strategies and collecting data on them. Data collection could include administering tests, observing students, and conducting surveys and interviews. In each chapter, you will be shown the types of actions that are aligned with that particular form of data collection.

3 **Analyze**: During the analysis phase, teachers carefully examine and analyze their data. The analysis could include observations of student interactions, the analysis of student work, the analysis of surveys and interviews, the analysis of pre-and post-tests, or the analysis of standardized achievement tests. Analysis during action research consists of a two-step process. First, action researchers should construct an objective description

of student performance. This description should be thorough, detailed, objective, and as free from judgments or inferences as possible. The more detached and objective the description, the better it lends itself to analysis and interpretation. Second, to multiply their observations action researchers should examine their data from different perspectives. Expanding your observations by shifting perspectives provides a wider basis for making interpretations in the next phase of your action research project. This can be accomplished by making comparisons and contrasts, by integrating different observations in different ways, and by viewing the data through different conceptual lenses. These techniques are explained and illustrated in various places throughout the book.

4   *Reflect*: The reflection phase consists of a three-step process. The first step is interpreting and explaining your observations. When interpreting your data, it is useful to generate as many plausible explanations as possible. You will find having a variety of explanations is helpful in the second step of the reflection process, which is developing new teaching strategies. Most new teaching strategies come from one of the following four sources: your past experience, data from your study, techniques shared by other teachers, or the educational literature. The third step of the reflection process is to justify your new teaching strategies by supporting them with data, best practice, educational research, or educational theory. Justification is critical because the thinking processes associated with developing a new strategy are often based on inspiration or intuitive thinking. Justification requires a more carefully reasoned rationale based on an analytical approach that links data, literature, and past experience. Throughout the book, you will be asked to engage in this three-step process of reflection when analyzing sample data.

Reflection 1.6

By systematically and thoroughly working through the four-step process illustrated in Figure 1.1, you can improve your ability to think objectively, to collect relevant data, to collaborate harmoniously with colleagues, and to cultivate your research persona. In the space below, describe a time when you have introduced a new teaching strategy, adjusted your teaching style, altered a lesson, or introduced a new resource to improve learning. Try to fit your description within the model for action research described above (plan, collect data, analyze, and reflect). To what degree does the model fit your description?

_____

_____

_____

---

5 Research Ethics

Action research requires a high level of ethical behavior. Like teachers, action researchers must not act in a way that causes either physical or psychological injury to a child. Usually, this means taking a very sensitive approach to sharing information collected from test scores, interviews, surveys, videotaped observations or other sources of data. The degree to which you have to be concerned about protecting your students' confidentiality is determined by your purpose for doing action research. For example, if the intent of your project is simply to inform your own instruction, and you do not plan to use your data outside of your school, then you need not be concerned about taking additional precautions to protect your students' privacy. In this case, your ethical obligations as a teacher are sufficient. As a rule, teachers are expected to exhibit great care in protecting their students' confidentiality.

However, your purpose for doing action research may broaden as your capabilities grow. If you decide to present or publish information from your classroom outside of your school district, then greater care must be taken to protect both the privacy and the rights of the child. Presenting and publishing action research can offer a significant benefit to the action researcher, possibly through an increase in professional status or in the form of pay for an inservice presentation. Unfortunately, there have been numerous past examples of researchers who took advantage of research participants to serve their own purposes. Therefore, extra considerations to protect the rights of the child are necessary.

Reflection 1.7

In the space below, describe two possible scenarios in which sharing information about a child in a public forum could cause harm.

_____

_____

_____

Reflection 1.8

In the following exercise put an "A" if the teacher's action research requires additional ethical considerations beyond those ordinarily taken by teachers as part of their professional responsibilities. Put an "N" if there is no need for additional procedures to protect the rights of the child.

_____ 1   Observe an individual child for the purpose of differentiating instruction.

_____ 2   Share the findings from your action research project with other fourth grade teachers in your school for the purpose of developing new instructional strategies.

_____ 3   Use your action research to do an inservice session for a group of teachers from a neighboring school district.

_____ 4   Publish an article on the effectiveness of a new strategy discovered through action research.

For those who plan to share their findings outside of their school district, additional steps are needed to ensure the rights of your research participants. For those of you who are already prepared to make such a step, this section will serve as a short introduction to those procedures. But please understand that the following is a *brief* introduction to research ethics and that the authors highly recommend additional reading. Those of you who are interested solely in improving your classroom instruction may want to skim this section. You can return to it later when you become interested in presenting or publishing your data.

To protect the rights of research participants, research universities have established Institutional Review Boards (IRB), which are governed by a set of federal regulations written to safeguard the rights of research participants. All research conducted at research universities for the purpose of wider dissemination, either through publications, presentations, websites or other electronic communication, must be approved by the IRB. Teachers who plan to disseminate their findings through publication or presentation and who are associated with a university through a graduate program should obtain permission for their action research project through the IRB. The IRB application requires researchers to describe in detail their research procedures and their plan to safeguard the rights of the participant. This includes describing the purpose of the study, the potential risks and benefits to the participants, the procedures for recruiting participants, and a plan for protecting the privacy of the participants.

Reflection 1.9

What differences do you see between your professional ethics as a teacher and your professional ethics as an action researcher?

_____

_____

_____

All research participants have the right to make an informed decision regarding their participation in a research study. Because action research often occurs as part of normal classroom activities within the prescribed school curriculum, asking for informed consent is somewhat different than other forms of research. It is the teacher's prerogative to decide what activities are beneficial for the child; therefore, the teacher has the right to determine whether or not a student should participate in a given activity. However, if the teacher desires to present data from the activity outside of her school district, then she must obtain informed consent from both student and parent.

In order for action research participants and their parents to give their informed consent, two elements must be present. *First, they must fully understand the nature of the research in which they are asked to participate.* The IRB requires that all research participants sign a letter of informed consent. The letter explains the procedures, any possible risks, and any potential benefits of the research. It also outlines the participants' rights, which includes their right not to participate and their right to quit the study at any time. When research participants are under the age of 18, both the student and a parent must each sign separate letters of consent. The letter should be written in simple, direct language to enable the participants to make an informed choice about their participation. Letters of consent should use language appropriate to the child's age level. For more information about the work of IRBs, you may consult the website of any university that conducts research. Detailed information on their procedures for protecting research participants will be posted.

Second, consent must be voluntary. Potential participants must feel free to refuse to participate, and they must be free to stop participating any time they choose. Enabling this choice can be a challenging issue. Previous research has clearly demonstrated that people will act in conflict with their desires in the presence of an authority figure. Because teachers are important authority figures for students and parents, asking your students to participate in an action research study may not really offer them much of a choice. Their desire to please you could cause them to hide their true feelings.

Fortunately, there are several remedies for avoiding any appearance of coercion when asking for your students' permission. The first is to ask them after the course or school year has ended, and they have received their final grades. This eliminates the possibility of any potential adverse consequence for their refusal. A variation of this approach is to have a third person (e.g., another teacher) ask your students for their permission. The consent forms could be collected and sealed in a manila envelope to be opened only after the school year has ended. This method achieves the same purpose as the first approach, while simultaneously eliminating the difficulty of contacting students after the course is over. A third way is to do your action research project in another teacher's classroom. In this case, coercion is eliminated because you are not working with your own students. To obtain comparable data on your students, the other teacher could reciprocate in your classroom. Thus, this approach makes it possible for you to use the data right away. However, there are disadvantages to this approach. First, working in another classroom requires a greater time commitment, and, second, you lose the benefit of collecting the data first-hand, which can be very instructive.

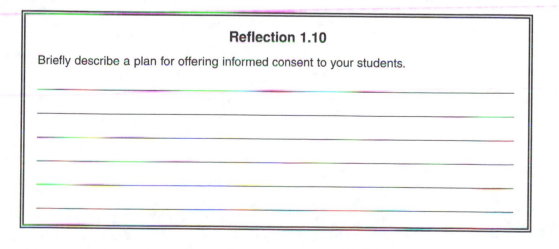

Reflection 1.10

Briefly describe a plan for offering informed consent to your students.

The IRB will probably not be a consideration for teachers who are not associated with a university. Schools that do not work with universities sometimes have a governing board that regulates research activity. Clearing your research project through such a board is highly desirable. Making public your intentions and getting prior permission will reassure parents about the nature of your work, legitimize your project among your colleagues, and may provide a source of support in case a problem arises during the project. If there is no official group that sanctions action research projects in your school, you should at least inform your principal and other administrators of your intentions.

It may also be helpful for you and other school personnel to know that university researchers are required to have IRB approval before collecting data in your school. To receive approval, they must obtain a letter of cooperation from a school official and include it in their IRB application.

6 Summary

This brief introductory chapter introduced you to action research by identifying action research as a form of qualitative research, by characterizing the differences between more formal educational research and action research, and by providing short definitions of action research. The idea of teachers as researchers extends back to the nineteenth century in the United States and is currently experiencing a resurgence of interest. Four benefits of action research for teachers include promoting student achievement, improving teaching strategies, enhancing professional development, and facilitating school improvement. Learning to think like a researcher means cultivating a research persona. Cultivating a research persona depends both on the systematic acquisition of research dispositions and habitually addressing problems through a four-step cycle: plan, collect data, analyze, and reflect. You will be asked to engage in this cycle of action research repeatedly throughout the book. Finally, the chapter concluded with a brief introduction to research ethics. Teachers in graduate programs who wish to present or publish their action research findings should gain permission for their research project from the Institutional Review Board. Teachers not affiliated with an IRB should ask permission of their students, the students' parents, the principal, and any local governing board, if one exists.

two
Planning an Action Research Project

The most meaningful image of action research derived from our teaching is a continuous, conscious attempt to seek increased meaning and direction in our lives with students, and in our own personal lives.

(Schubert & Schubert, cited in Hobson, 2001, p. 4)

1 Introduction

The aim of this chapter is to help you plan your action research project. Planning involves thinking about what you want to improve, how you will go about it, and how you will evaluate what you've done. In the following sections, the process of planning an action research study is organized into four steps. The first step involves formulating an initial research question by reflecting on puzzling student behaviors, pressing problems, or needs identified by your school district. The second step is to search for a new teaching strategy through your observations of students, your dialog with other teachers, and your engagement in professional development activities. The third step requires a search of the educational literature for the purpose of further exploring new strategies and finding research evidence that supports their use in the classroom. Fourth and finally, you need to consider what method of data collection you will need to evaluate the effectiveness of your teaching strategies.

2 Formulating a Research Question

The very first step in starting an action research project is to formulate a research question based on a topic, issue, or problem that you would like to investigate. A research question is essential to an action research study. It gives purpose and direction to designing the study, choosing the research methods, and interpreting the research findings. The entire process of planning and conducting an action research study will be influenced by the question you choose at the outset.

Since conducting an action research study will require considerable time and focus; you should try to pick a research question that is worthy of the additional effort it will require. Reflect on your experience in the classroom and think about student behaviors that have raised your curiosity, pressing problems that need to be solved, needs identified by your school's improvement plan, or a new teaching strategy you would like to try. The problems, issues, and innovations that are part of your everyday classroom interactions make the best sources of action research questions.

If you have difficulty thinking of a question, you may stimulate the process by simply watching your students more closely. The additional information gained through observations could help you locate your topic. Here are six techniques for more systematically observing your students:

1   Observe for unexplained, puzzling or unusual behaviors.
2   Observe the behaviors of individual children.
3   Explore diversity.
4   Keep a journal.
5   Examine the curriculum.
6   Reflect on your teaching.

Observing Unexplained, Puzzling, or Unusual Behaviors

Your action research project could begin with just a vague desire to improve or a sense of dissatisfaction with the status quo. These feelings can be important indicators of classroom interactions that could be improved. For example, in a high school English class the teacher is frustrated by a lack of participation during the discussion. The teacher assigns a short story for the class to read over night as a homework assignment. As part of their homework, the class has to answer a set of questions on a worksheet. When the students come to class the next day, the teacher asks them a series of questions about the short story. Four or five students respond to the teacher's questions; the rest sit quietly or talk among themselves at inappropriate times or withdraw completely. This pattern is repeated among many classes, except some days when even fewer students participate or other days when the class is noisier and more off task.

Reflection 2.1

What kinds of questions would these observations raise in your mind?

_____

_____

_____

_____

Observe an Individual Child

Another approach to finding a topic would be to focus your observations on an individual child. For instance, suppose you made the following observations about Alicia. Alicia is a third grader reading at the second grade level. Her behavior and expressive language can be impulsive due to her ADHD (Attention Deficit Hyperactivity Disorder). She has difficulty self-starting, attending to tasks, and usually requires teacher support to complete her work. However, she responds well to attention and is eager to please teachers.

Reflection 2.2

What kinds of questions would these observations raise in your mind?

Explore Diversity

Given the increasingly diverse U.S. school population, making observations related to the language use of diverse students, their performance in class, and their standardized achievement test scores could be a worthwhile starting point for an action research study. For instance, imagine you have three Hispanic students in your classroom. They've lived in the USA for over two years, participate in a pullout program for supplemental instruction in English, and they appear to speak English well. Their grades are average, but their standardized test scores are well below average.

Reflection 2.3

What kinds of questions would these observations raise in your mind?

Keep a Journal

Keeping a journal is a way of keeping a record of your reflections about your teaching. Examining your journal reflections over a period of time can suggest possibilities for action research. For instance, suppose you kept a series of journal entries during an inquiry-based science unit. As you read through the journal entries, you notice numerous entries in which students are unsure what they should be doing and are late with their assignments.

Reflection 2.4

What kinds of questions would these observations raise in your mind?

_____

_____

_____

_____

Examine the Curriculum

Examining the curriculum could also yield some possibilities for an action research project. One approach would be to analyze your school's standardized achievement test scores. For example, what if the standardized test scores for computational math showed a consistent dip among fourth graders over a three-year period? Each year the scores are relatively high in third grade, dip in fourth grade, and then rise again in fifth grade.

Reflection 2.5

What kinds of questions would these observations raise in your mind?

_____

_____

_____

_____

Reflect on Your Teaching

Now try thinking about observations you have made of your students. Do you have questions about student behaviors, student performance, or your interactions with students?

Reflection 2.6

Think of some observations you have made of a child or make some observations below. Jot down three questions those observations have raised in your mind. Explain the basis for your questions.

_____

_____

_____

_____

_____

_____

_____

---

3 Searching for a Strategy

Once you have decided on an initial question, the second step of planning your action research question project is finding or creating a new strategy to improve learning. Trying new strategies is at the heart of action research. Each time you try a new strategy and evaluate it through data collection, it deepens your insight into your practice. A successfully implemented strategy is an indication that you have diagnosed the problem accurately and that similar strategies may also prove beneficial. An ineffective strategy may be an indication that either the problem was misdiagnosed or the strategy wasn't implemented appropriately.

To some degree, finding new teaching strategies depends on inspiration. The sources of inspiration for action researchers are very similar to those for other researchers. Researchers tend to draw inspiration from their previous experiences, their everyday observations, their reading, their conversation with colleagues, and their findings from previous research. Similarly, inspiration for teachers engaged in action research may come from our daily concerns in our classroom, talking to other teachers, reading the educational literature, or engaging in professional development activities.

For example, on p. 16, a secondary English teacher was frustrated by a lack of participation. She might have asked herself any of the following questions:

1   Is the reading level of the short story too high?
2   Are students sufficiently interested in the short stories?
3   Are students practiced in higher-level thinking skills?
4   Could I ask better questions?
5   Is there a way I could better motivate my students?
6   Is there a better way to organize the discussion?
7   Are expectations clear?

To answer these questions, the teacher must determine a course of action that either addresses all of these possibilities, some of these possibilities, or at least one of these possibilities. Consequently, she must search for multiple strategies that address multiple aspects of the problem, or find a strategy to address the single most important problem. Three sources of new strategies are introduced in the following sections. These include observing students and their work, getting strategies from other teachers, and participating in a professional development program.

Observing Students and Their Work

One approach to generating new strategies is through direct observation of student performance or the products of their work. By watching student performance or studying their products, you can often directly see where the student is having difficulty and then develop a strategy that directly addresses it.

Reflection 2.7

(a) Based on the teacher's observations on p. 16, which of the six questions above do you think is more likely to be the cause of the problem? (You may choose more than one.) Explain why you think so.

_____

_____

_____

_____

(b) Based on those observations, what strategies might you suggest as part of an action research project?

_____

_____

_____

_____

Reflection 2.8

After you have decided on a specific strategy to use in your action research project, you may want to tweak your research question. Use one of the approaches described on pp. 16–20 to create a research question that would address the specific strategy you plan to implement, as well as the subject of the investigation.

_____

_____

_____

Other Teachers

A second source of new strategies is other teachers. Getting ideas from other teachers can happen in all sorts of ways: through casual conversation, by asking teachers whom you respect, or through a more structured collaboration. By participating in a teacher study group or data assessment team, teachers can regularly share their findings and strategies from their action research studies. More detailed information on teacher collaboration can be found in Chapter 9.

Reflection 2.9

(a) Based on the teacher's observations on p. 16, what kinds of questions might you ask other teachers in order to find new strategies for your action research project?

_____

_____

_____

(b) Do you have a chance to regularly engage with other teachers in analyzing student data and sharing strategies? How often and what do you discuss?

_____

_____

_____

Professional Development

A third approach for acquiring strategies is through a program of professional development. This approach often occurs in conjunction with a systematic effort to improve curriculum and instruction on a school-wide basis. The strategies in this program may be based on a previous analysis of student achievement to find the gaps in student performance.

Reflection 2.10

Based on the teacher's observations on p. 16, what kinds of professional development sessions might be helpful for trying to improve class participation?

_____

_____

_____

_____

Reflection 2.11

Are you currently engaged in a program of professional development at your school that cultivates a specific set of teaching skills? What new strategies have you learned?

_____

_____

_____

---

4 Searching the Educational Literature

The third step in planning your action research project involves conducting a search of the educational literature. A literature search provides two primary benefits. First, for teachers who are interested in expanding their repertoire of teaching techniques, the educational literature offers yet another rich source of new strategies to explore. Second, for teachers interested in establishing their practice as research-based, educational literature can provide evidence to justify the use of either new or existing strategies. Evidence from the previous literature combined with the results from your action research projects makes a powerful combination for justifying the use of instructional strategies.

The educational literature consists of a wide variety of information contributed by a diverse group of educators, including teachers, administrators, policy makers, and researchers. Because this information can vary in both purpose and quality, we will compare three different sources of information in this section, including educational journals, educational databases, and other sources of information such as the Internet. We will also offer some guidance on enhancing your ability to find and read articles from educational journals.

Educational Journals

Most journal articles can be classified as belonging to either primary or secondary literature. Primary literature consists of articles that report on research studies. The main purpose of primary literature is to provide evidence for using a particular process, for understanding thought processes, or for explaining an educational phenomenon. In this type of article, there will be a group of research participants, a method for collecting data, findings from the data, and a discussion of what the findings mean. Examples of articles from primary literature might include a comparison of methods for teaching fractions, a description of a child's thinking while reading, or an explanation of how a particular school has created such positive relationships with parents. The methods for these studies would include observing students, recording student comments, comparing students' test scores, or interviewing and surveying participants.

In contrast to primary literature, secondary literature makes recommendations about what should be done, gives advice on how a process could be done, or explains how a process works. These recommendations are based on findings established in primary literature. In this type of article, knowledge gained from primary literature is applied to educational settings. Examples from secondary literature might include an article that recommends strategies for teaching fractions, explains the importance of asking children questions about their reading, or offers suggestions for ways to promote more positive relationships with parents.

Thus, there is a relationship between primary and secondary literature. Primary literature seeks to find the best approaches to teaching and learning: secondary literature uses those findings to make recommendations to educators interested in improving their practice.

Reflection 2.12

Several examples of primary and secondary literature are given below. Identify examples of primary literature with a "P" and examples of secondary literature with an "S."

_____ 1   This article compares the pre- and post-test scores of two groups of students to determine which group improved the most. Both groups were taught by the same teacher, who used a whole class discussion with one group and a whole class discussion combined with cooperative learning with the second group. The findings show the second group participated more in class and wrote better essays.

_____ 2   This article presents a list of reasons why cooperative learning is an effective teaching method. It then summarizes the five principles of cooperative learning and gives examples of how teachers might use them to increase participation and student learning.

_____ 3   This article describes the key elements of creating and leading discussions in literature circles. It discusses possible benefits of using literature circles and warns readers about potential pitfalls. The article concludes with a sample lesson plan of a teacher who has used literature circles effectively for the past five years.

_____ 4   This article consists of survey results from 150 teachers who have used literature circles in their instruction. The findings show what teachers have found to be the benefits, limitations, and the most optimal situations to use literature circles.

_____ 5   In this article, the author reports on her interviews and observations of 10 principals as they worked through the process of evaluating their teachers. The findings describe common assessment beliefs and practices among principals. Implications for future practice are suggested.

_____ 6   In this article, the author draws on the previous research literature to explain the importance of using manipulatives in math instruction. The author describes situations in which math manipulatives are most effective and provides tips from teachers who have used math manipulatives successfully.

Reading Research Articles

Just as educational journal articles vary in type, they also vary in their readability. Articles from secondary literature are generally easier to read than primary articles, probably because the main purpose of secondary literature is to make recommendations intended to improve classroom teaching. Thus, the context of the article, the terminology used, and the issues addressed by the authors will be familiar to teachers. In comparison, articles from primary literature are written from a less familiar context and require more background knowledge than secondary articles. They generally have a much narrower focus and require more knowledge of the technical terms and procedures associated with research.

One way to make research articles more readable is to take a Masters level course in educational research, which should provide help with reading research. However, for those who have not or do not plan to take such a course, the following strategies can help. First and foremost, it is important to find research articles that interest you. Few are interested in research for its own sake: most of us are interested in research in the specific subject areas in which we have a high interest, are highly involved, and possess some expertise. Your expertise as an educator is an invaluable aid for reading research. Second, it is important to understand that there is considerable variation in the readability of research studies. Some are highly technical and are best suited for highly trained and experienced researchers. Others are shorter with less complicated methods that apply more directly to the interests and needs of classroom teachers. It is important to find research journals that are readable, given your current level of training.

Third, it may be helpful to know that researchers do not necessarily read studies in a linear fashion from beginning to end. A better strategy is to read the Introduction, which makes an initial broad statement of the problem within its real world context. Then read the Discussion, which summarizes the results of the study and interprets their significance for real-world settings. Both of these sections provide broad overviews of the study and its relationship to an applied setting. Reading them first should provide you with a global understanding of the study that will enable you to understand the more technical information treated in the literature review, methods, and findings sections found in the interior of the study. Even if you experience difficulty there, you will still find your understanding of the introduction and discussion useful for future reading.

Fourth and finally, try not to fret too much about the meaning of statistical symbols. Many teachers worry that if they do not understand the statistical references, they will miss the meaning of the study. It may comfort you to know that the significance of the statistical analysis is always stated in natural language, e.g., "Group A performed significantly better than Group B." While it is true that understanding the statistical references will deepen your grasp of the study, it will not necessarily prevent you from understanding its general import. If you are experiencing significant difficulty with interpreting the study, it is more likely due to your lack of familiarity with previous research studies on the same topic. By their very nature, research studies are highly compressed, so their interpretation depends on considerable background knowledge. But there is good news. If you persist in your reading of research studies, you will find that many foundational ideas are repeated from study to study. With each new study, your understanding of a line of research continues to grow and thus the studies become easier to read.

Reflection 2.13

(a) Use the spaces below to reflect on your own reading habits. Are you currently reading from the educational literature? What types of articles do you like to read? How often do you read them?

_____

_____

_____

_____

(b) Do you read articles from primary or secondary literature? How could you expand the range of articles you are reading? List a few strategies below.

_____

_____

_____

_____

Electronic Databases

In recent years, libraries have begun to store an increasing number of journals in electronic databases. Electronic databases offer several advantages for action researchers. First, they often provide greater access to the educational research. Typing in a single search term can yield far more information in far less time than would be possible by searching through individual journals. Second, they are often more convenient. Increasingly, databases offer a full text of the article that can be downloaded from a computer, thus eliminating or reducing the amount of commuting to the library. In addition, a few are freely available on the Internet. However, in many cases, this only applies to articles published in recent years. In addition, most databases are not free and can only be accessed by members of an organization, such as a university library. Since electronic databases vary in their information sources, accessibility, and convenience, it is often helpful to use more than one to obtain all the information you need. Below is a brief description of four different databases. These are intended only as a sample introduction.

- *ERIC (Education Resources Information Center).* ERIC is a comprehensive educational database that includes journal articles, books, research syntheses, conference papers, technical reports, policy papers, and other education-related materials that date back to 1966. ERIC users include education researchers, teachers, librarians, administrators, education policymakers, instructors and students in teacher-preparation programs, parents, the media and business communities, and the general public. ERIC offers a broad variety of education resources that are freely available online and their collection of full text articles is expanding.

- *Google Scholar*. Like ERIC, Google Scholar is also freely available on line; therefore, it provides an alternative to ERIC. However, it is not limited to education articles, so your searches may yield articles that have little interest to you. Google Scholar covers a great range of topical areas, consisting of full-text journal articles, technical reports, preprints, theses, books, and other documents. It is probably strongest in the sciences, particularly medicine, and secondarily in the social sciences.

- *Education Full Text (Wilson Web)*. Education Full Text covers a wide range of educational topics from an international range of English-language periodicals, monographs, and yearbooks. The advantage of Education Full Text is the number of full text articles available through this database. The entire database extends back as far as 1983: Full text articles from over 350 journals are available as far back as 1996. Education Full Text provides a good option for those who would prefer to download their articles. However, gaining access requires affiliation with a university or other organization.

- *JSTOR (Journal Storage)*. Includes archives of over one thousand leading academic journals across the humanities, social sciences, and sciences, as well as select monographs and other materials valuable for academic work. This database enables retrieval of full text articles from the past; however, it does not carry more current articles. The most recently published issues (past 3–5 years) are not available. Thus, JSTOR serves as a storage house for articles over 3–5 years old. Many of them are full text.

Reflection 2.14

For each of the following situations, describe which one or which combination of databases you would use to conduct your literature search.

(a) Which sources of information (including journals, books, databases, etc.) would you use if you were a teacher who was not affiliated with a university through a graduate program and if you did not live very close to a university library? Please give a rationale for your choices.

_____

_____

_____

_____

(b) Which sources of information (including journals, books, databases, etc.) would you use if you were a teacher who was affiliated with a university graduate program, but primarily through a distance learning program? In this case, it is not convenient for you to commute to the university library? Please give a rationale for your choices.

_____

_____

_____

_____

(c) Which sources of information (including journals, books, databases, etc.) would you use if you were a teacher who was affiliated with a university through a graduate program and lived within easy access to the university library? Please give a rationale for your choices.

_____

_____

_____

_____

Searching Databases

To use databases effectively, you must be able to conduct successful searches. The ERIC databases will be used to introduce a few basic ideas about searches. The key to a successful search is an effective keyword, such as the title or the author of a journal article or book. More often, you will not know the author or title of the work. In that case, a successful search depends on finding a keyword based on relevance. These would be single words or phrases that describe the topic, such as "early childhood education." There are two potential problems using a keyword based on relevance. First, the keyword may not find a match in the database. Sometimes the terms researchers use to frame a problem are different than those found in the educational literature. A second problem is the amount of information the keyword may elicit. If the keyword is too common, you may locate more articles than you can possibly utilize. For example, a recent search using the keyword "cooperative learning" yielded 13,784 responses.

One approach to finding relevant keywords is to use the ERIC thesaurus, which is easily visible near the top of the search page. Selecting the thesaurus will lead you to a list of general descriptors. Selecting one of these will lead you to another list and so on. For example, selecting the descriptor Educational Process: Classroom Perspectives leads to another list of descriptors. Selecting Study Habits from that list will lead to another list. Continuing with this search, successive descriptors were selected, including Reading Habits, Reading Motivation, Reading Strategies, Reading Skills, and finally, Functional Literacy. A search for Functional Literacy elicited 1277 postings.

To retrieve these postings, select "Start an ERIC Search." There are two types of ERIC searches "Basic" and "Advanced." The "Advanced" Search offers several additional features over the "Basic" Search. First, it allows you to add more descriptors to your search. By adding Reading Skills as a second descriptor, the number of postings for Functional Literacy is reduced from 1277 to 77, a much more manageable number within a more focused topic area. Another way to reduce the number of postings further is to target more recent publications (e.g., since 2000) and limit those to articles for which the full text is available. If those additional options are selected for the search, the number of postings is reduced to 10. This number can be reduced even further by specifying the type of publication (e.g., journal, book, ERIC document, etc.) and the education level.

Reflection 2.15

Make a list of search terms that are relevant to a topic that interests you.

_____

_____

_____

_____

Other Sources of Information

There are numerous other sources of educational information available on the Internet, including lesson plans, sample tests, and webquests, as well as many others. Often these sources of information can be very helpful to teachers, especially if you need to acquire an initial understanding of a topic very quickly. However, the usefulness of this information is limited because it has not undergone the same quality control process that applies to educational books and journals. For example, the information you find on a website has probably not been reviewed by other educators before it is posted. Therefore, this type of information does not provide a credible source of research-based evidence to support the introduction of new teaching strategies. This type of support must come from educational journals that are peer-reviewed.

However, judicious use of information found on the Internet can lead to the discovery of more research-based information. For instance, a website may provide citations or a reference list that could give you important background information, and provide information that would lead to stronger sources of evidence, such as articles published in educational journals. The published information found in the educational journal would provide the supporting evidence for justifying your strategies, not the information found on the website.

Reflection 2.16

Google the search terms you listed in Reflection 2.15. Did your search lead you to any educational journal articles? Give examples.

_____

_____

_____

_____

---

5 Selecting the Methods

A final consideration when planning action research are the methods of data collection you will use to collect your data. The method you choose should complement your research question. For example, if the purpose of the research study is to examine question-asking strategies, participation patterns, and other teacher—student interactions, making observations might be the best approach. Similarly, investigating the behavior of an individual child might best be accomplished through observations. If the purpose of the study is to find out how students, teachers, administrators, or parents, feel about a change in school policy, a new teaching method, a new school procedure, or changes caused by a recent event; then interviews or surveys are probably the best approaches to that topic. If the purpose of the study is to determine gains in student learning, to find gaps in the curriculum, to compare the effectiveness of different teaching strategies, or to compare the learning gains of individual students to the whole class, then student work or test scores might be the best source of data.

Each method of data collection will yield different insights, and each has different advantages and limitations. For example, observations can yield first-hand information about student performance but can be very subjective. Interviews and surveys can provide insight into the perceptions and opinions of research participants, but do not necessarily reflect what has actually happened. Testing provides objective data concerning student performance, but may provide less insight about new strategies than observations.

Each research method should be valued for the unique insight it can offer regarding a particular problem. Each research method provides a different piece of the puzzle so that none are superior or inferior measures of "truth." As you become a more experienced teacher researcher, you will gain a deeper understanding of what each method can and cannot do. Here is a brief overview of the methods presented in Chapters 3–8:

1   *Observing students and student work* has the advantage of offering the action researcher a great deal of flexibility while collecting data. Since teachers constantly make observations of their students, the methodology is relatively familiar and comfortable. However, action researchers must be aware that they carry assumptions, which may cause them to miss important aspects of the data. The more systematically the observations are made, the more objective and reliable they are. This source of data can complement other sources, like classroom assessment data, surveys, and interviews.

2   *Observing teachers* can provide an objective record of the types of teacher talk in the classroom. However, it can be difficult to know whether or not the teacher discourse moves are appropriate without knowing the teacher's intentions. Interview data could supply this information.

3   *Surveys* have an advantage over interviews because they reach more participants and therefore can give action researchers a much larger view of the issue. Action researchers can be more confident that the findings are representative of a larger group of people than interviews. Like interviews, they are limited to the subjective perceptions of the participants. So it is important to remember than neither interview nor survey data can claim to represent the actual facts of the matter, but only the facts as the participants believe them to be. Combining survey and interview research can give the action researcher both breadth and depth of insight.

4   *Interviews* can provide more in-depth insights into the participants' thinking than surveys. They enable the researcher personal contact with the participant and provide an opportunity to ask follow-up questions. However, because interviews are time-consuming, they are usually limited to just a few participants. In addition, interviews are limited to the perceptions of the participants, which may or may not represent the actual situation.

5   *Standardized test analysis* provides an objective measure of student achievement in comparison to their peers. Results can give broad indications about student achievement and the effectiveness of the overall curriculum. However, it is sometimes difficult to determine which specific teaching strategies resulted in improved student performance because standardized tests are generally given no more than once per year. Furthermore, the results from a fall test may not be available for weeks or months, thus further delaying the opportunity to evaluate teaching strategies. In sum, standardized achievement tests provide little feedback on day-to-day instruction.

6   *Pre- and post-test data* enable teachers to use classroom tests as a source of data and a means to develop new teaching strategies. They provide a broad view of student achievement. To link to strategies teachers must examine specific questions and their relationship to specific learning goals.

Reflection 2.17

Here is a set of research questions. Identify the method or methods you think would provide the best data by putting an "O" for observation, an "I" for interview, an "S" for Survey, and a "T" for test score. You may use more than one if you think it will better answer the research question.

_____ 1   Would asking higher level questions improve the quality of student participation?

_____ 2   Would differentiating instruction increase the achievement of special needs learners in my class?

_____ 3   How do students perceive the introduction of manipulatives into the math curriculum?

_____ 4   Will implementing cooperative learning increase student learning in my class?

_____ 5   Will implementing cooperative learning improve the quality of interactions in my class?

_____ 6   What kind of support do parents provide for their children's emerging literacy skills?

Utilizing a variety of data sources can enable the researcher to assemble a composite answer that is deeper, more informed, and addresses more aspects of the research question than any single source could. Even on the occasions when the findings from different data sources are incongruous, trying to integrate the findings from different data sources can prompt us to think more deeply. To integrate different forms of data into a composite picture requires understanding the contribution and limitations of each form of data as described above.

Following are two examples of different ways to combine data sources. These are intended to serve only as an illustration of a wide variety of possibilities, depending on your research question, participants, and the available resources:

1   *Standardized Tests and Analyzing Student Work.* Using standardized tests with student work combines objective evidence of student learning with an ongoing analysis skill development. One approach is to select two or three representative students based on their standardized achievement scores or other testing data for the purpose of studying their work deeply. The analysis of student work is intended to develop strategies that apply to the rest of the class. Newly implemented strategies are evaluated by their impact on both student work and the students' standardized test scores or pre-and post-tests (Langer et al., 2003).
2   *Observing Students, Survey, and Interview.* This approach to action research is intended to supplement the teacher's observations of students with observational data that examines their perception of the process. Surveys could provide input from the entire class or a larger group of students. That data could be further illuminated by interviewing three to six of the students in depth. These students could be selected as representatives of subgroups within the class, based on ability, gender, ethnicity, or some other classification.

In the previous sections, we considered four steps for planning action research, including selecting a topic, searching for strategies, searching the educational literature, and selecting a method. In this section, you will modify an initial research question based on a literature search, select the methods you will use, and then explain why you chose those methods. In this section, these three considerations will be integrated into a single research question.

Reflection 2.18

For example, on p. 16, the teacher observed a lack of participation. This led to a string of questions, such as: Are the students motivated or could I organize my discussions differently? Identifying those initial questions initiates a literature search to find new strategies. When the search reveals that cooperative learning groups can motivate students, the teacher's initial question expands to: Will letting students discuss in small groups before the large group discussion improve class participation? Put a check by the data collection method below that would be the most appropriate for answering this research question.

_____ Observations   _____ Interview

_____ Survey   _____ Test scores

Explain why you chose your answer(s).

_____

_____

_____

Reflection 2.19

(a) On p. 17, Alicia was observed to have difficulty with impulsive language, attending to tasks, and completing tasks without the help of the teacher. This led to an initial question: How can Alicia become more autonomous? Consulting with other teachers and searching the literature has led to the idea of teaching Alicia some cognitive strategies that would help her become more independent. Use this information to write one or more research questions in the space below.

_____

_____

_____

(b) Put a check by the data collection method below that would be the most appropriate for answering this research question.

_____ Observations   _____ Interview

_____ Survey   _____ Test scores

Explain why you chose your answer(s).

_____

_____

_____

Reflection 2.20

(a) On p. 17, a discrepancy was observed between the classroom performance and standardized achievement tests scores of three Hispanic students who recently arrived in the United States. This led to an initial question: Are these students as proficient in English as they appear in the classroom? Several strategies were suggested by the literature on multicultural education. They included speaking more slowly when giving directions, using more visual aids, and making the instruction more relevant to the previous experience of the three students. Use this information to write one or more research questions in the space below.

_____

_____

_____

(b) Put a check by the data collection method below that would be the most appropriate for answering this research question. You may use more than one.

_____ Observations   _____ Interview

_____ Survey   _____ Test scores

Explain why you chose your answer(s).

_____

_____

_____

Reflection 2.21

(a) On p. 18, several journal entries noted that students were unsure what to do and were turning in their assignments late during an inquiry-based unit in science. This led to an initial question: Do these students need more instructional guidance? Conversations with other teachers suggested several strategies for scaffolding student learning. They included using rubrics, exemplars from previous classes, and the setting of short-term goals. Use this information to write one or more research questions in the space below.

_____

_____

_____

(b) Put a check by the data collection method below that would be the most appropriate for answering this research question. You may use more than one.

_____ Observations   _____ Interview

_____ Survey   _____ Test scores

Explain why you chose your answer(s).

_____

_____

_____

Reflection 2.22

(a) On p. 18, a dip in computational math scores was observed in the fourth grade achievement test scores. This led to an initial question: Are more strategies or different strategies needed to teach computational math at the fourth grade level? A recent professional development program advocated the use of a daily practice problem as a way of improving computational skills. Use this information to write one or more research questions in the space below.

_____

_____

_____

(b) Put a check by the data collection method below that would be the most appropriate for answering this research question. You may use more than one

_____ Observations   _____ Interview

_____ Survey   _____ Test scores

Explain why you chose your answer(s).

_____

_____

_____

6 Summary

The aim of this chapter was to help you plan an action research project. The first step would be to formulate a research question. Formulating a research question is a critical initial step to conducting action research. The research question provides an explicit purpose that guides and shapes an action research project through each stage of the process. It requires integrating what you have learned from your observations, your search for new strategies, and your consideration of the methods.

The second step would be to increase your awareness of student behaviors through more systematic approaches to observation. Start looking for student responses, behaviors, or problems that arouse your curiosity. There are several approaches you could take.

1   Observe for unexplained, puzzling or unusual behaviors.
2   Observe the behaviors of individual children.
3   Explore diversity.
4   Keep a journal.
5   Examine the curriculum.
6   Search for new strategies.

The third step would be to look for strategies that address the situation you have identified. Trying and identifying new strategies is a critical element of action research. Three approaches were discussed in this chapter: examining student work, sharing strategies among teachers, and learning strategies through a professional development program.

The fourth step would be to search the educational literature to discover new strategies and to find evidence of their effectiveness. Journal articles, which can be divided into primary and secondary literature, can be found in university libraries and educational databases. A variety of different databases can aid you in your work. While some information is online and free, having access to a university library is still a great advantage.

The fifth step would be to select suitable methods. Some methods are more suited to answer particular questions than others. Data on classroom interactions can be collected through observations. Data on perceptions and attitudes is best collected through surveys and interviews. Gains in student achievement are best measured through testing and other forms of student work.

Part II
Making Observations

Part II consists of two chapters, each of which addresses making systematic classroom observations. Chapter 3 describes how to make observations of students, including observations of their behaviors, samples of their work, and their talking. Chapter 4 describes how to observe teachers as they interact with students. The primary advantage of observational data is that it can more directly suggest specific teaching strategies than test data. However, unless observations are made in a systematic and controlled fashion, they may be highly subjective and provide little insight.

three
Observing Students and Their Work

If the potential of the notion of practical knowledge, knowledge-in-action, personal practical knowledge, or teacher knowledge is to be realized, all who would study it face an obligation to seriously face the fact they are studying notions of knowledge and, as such, must work through matters of warrant and justification.

(Gary Fenstermacher, 1994, p. 49)

1 Introduction

The aim of this chapter is to show teachers how to observe students and their work in ways that enhance the development of new teaching strategies. Daily classroom observations are an important source of data for teachers. Observations of students can provide insight into discovering the causes of unexpected patterns of student behavior. More specifically, they can indicate the level of student involvement, the degree to which students are involved in higher level thinking, and the quality of student interactions. Methods of observation can range from open-ended queries to checklists of targeted student behaviors. Examples would include observing students while completing a task, while talking in groups, while working on a project, or while performing a skill. Student work can also be examined by noting strengths or weaknesses in student writing, student tests, and patterns of student problem solving. Finally, student talk can also be studied to determine response patterns, as well as the quantity and quality of student interactions.

A primary advantage of making observations is their value when developing new teaching strategies, especially when tasks are open-ended and require higher level thinking skills. Observations offer the following advantages for teachers:

1   Since teachers are highly familiar with observing students, the methodology is relatively familiar and comfortable.
2   They provide teachers a great deal of flexibility while collecting data.
3   They are very helpful for generating teaching strategies.
4   They complement other data sources very well, e.g., surveys, interviews, and standardized achievement tests. For example, analyzing standardized test data can help teachers identify a problem area. Observations of students and their work can provide valuable information for developing new strategies.

A potential limitation to using observational data is bias, i.e., the action researcher sees what she wants to see. To compensate for this potential problem, teachers also need to be aware that they bring assumptions to what they observe, and their assumptions may cause them to miss important aspects of the data. To avoid overlooking significant aspects of your data and to increase the objectivity of your observations, examine the data from as many perspectives as possible in as systematic and thorough a way as possible. One suggestion would be to put aside your rubric and examine student work with a completely fresh set of eyes. Simply glancing at a students' work or casually making observations is not likely to lead to any new insights.

This chapter is organized into four major parts. The first of these parts illustrates the importance of observing in a systematic way with an awareness of how your assumptions influence what you see. The information in the first sections can be applied to all of the three following parts. The second part describes how to systematically make open-ended observations of students as they engage in problem solving, interact in groups, or engage in any other observable activity. The third part describes how closely observing student work products (e.g., writing, artwork, a project) can lead to new strategies. The fourth section of the chapter describes how to make observations by recording student talking with a checklist, a journal entry, or an audio or video recording.

2 Making Careful Observations

The most important point to make about observations is that they need to be made carefully and systematically.

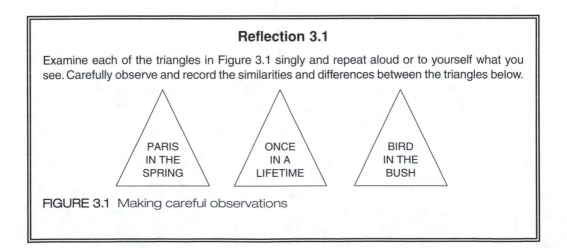

Reflection 3.1

Examine each of the triangles in Figure 3.1 singly and repeat aloud or to yourself what you see. Carefully observe and record the similarities and differences between the triangles below.

PARIS IN THE SPRING

ONCE IN A LIFETIME

BIRD IN THE BUSH

FIGURE 3.1 Making careful observations

(a) In what ways are these triangles different?

_____

_____

_____

(b) In what ways are they similar?

_____

_____

_____

(c) In your description of the triangles, did you note that each triangle contained an extra word? Go back and look at each triangle more carefully. What is the extra word in the first one? _____ Second one? _____ Third one? _____

(d) If you didn't notice that there are duplicate words in each triangle, don't feel bad. Very few people read these triangles correctly the first time. Why do you think this is so?

_____

_____

_____

_____

(e) Of what significance is this for conducting action research?

_____

_____

_____

Reflection 3.2

Let's try another example. Look at the Figure 3.2 and then jot down a description of what you see.

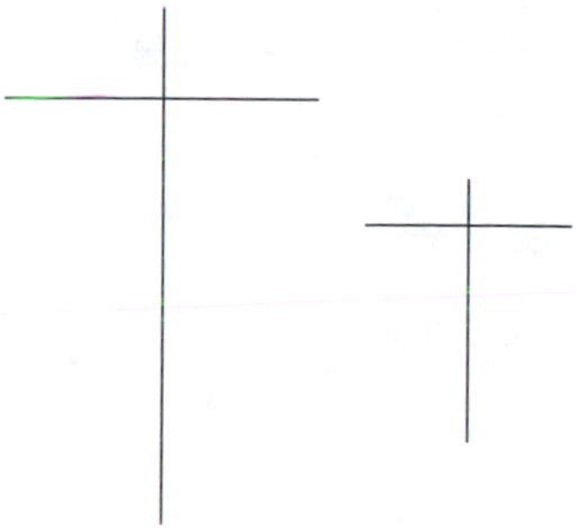

FIGURE 3.2 Two crossed lines

(Continued)

(Continued)

_____

_____

_____

(b) What did you write about this figure? Most people would say, "Two lines, one longer than the other that cross perpendicularly." Is that what you said? What if a different set of assumptions were guiding your observations? For example, let's assume the two lines actually represent a rendering of telephone poles. View the drawing once more. Do you see two telephone poles? Now how would you describe the drawing?

Description _____

_____

_____

_____

(c) Most people respond that they now see the two telephone poles, one being farther away from the other. Notice how the perception changes when you change your assumption. How can your assumptions shape your observations?

_____

_____

_____

_____

The examples above were intended to make two important points about making observations. First, unless observations are made in a careful, controlled, and systematic way, much valuable information can be lost. Second, our assumptions influence what we see. So it is critically important to be as aware as possible of the assumptions that guide our thinking. In the following sections, three different approaches to making observations will be discussed: observing students, their work, and their talk. Each approach offers a systematic way to make observations, but each is guided by slightly different assumptions, which make them distinctly different from each other.

3 Steps in Observational Research

When making observations about students, their work, or their talk, teachers follow similar steps. An overview of these steps is given below:

1 Plan
   (a) Establish the goals of the project. State your goals in the form of a research question. What is it that you want to learn from your observations?
   (b) Select your participants. Do you want to observe a single student, a group of students, a classroom of students, or students as they move around a school building? Explain the relationship between your participants and the research question.

   (c) Define the context of your observation. At what times and in what place will you be
        observing? What will you be looking for?
2 Collect data
   (a) Collect data through notetaking, videotaping, journal writing, or using a checklist.
3 Analyze
   (a) As you conduct the observation, withhold judgment. Record factual information. Try
        to avoid making inferences or imposing your judgment on the data.
4 Reflect
   (a) Interpret your observations.
   (b) Develop new teaching strategies.
   (c) Justify the teaching strategies.
   (d) Produce a summary report.

4 Observing Students

Observing students consists of watching students as they engage in some behavior.
Example investigations might include watching how students use reference materials in
the library, watching students solve math problems, watching how students build relationships in cooperative group settings, observing the activity at a learning or reading
center, or observing the behavior of a gifted child while engaged in differentiated
instruction. While this approach allows a wide variety of open-ended inquiries, it is
imperative that observations be systematic and objective. In other words, action
researchers must be careful to avoid simply seeing what they want to see or what they
have been conditioned to see. In the following sections, you will learn how to make systematic, objective observations.

Plan: Research Question

Like the other forms of action research, the plan for an observational study begins with
the formulation of a research question. The research question will serve as a guide and
organizing force for your observations. For example, the following research question was
developed for an action research study investigating the effectiveness of allowing students
more choices: "Does giving students more choices about their reading assignments
improve the quality of student participation during discussion?" The question suggests
that the action taken during the study will be allowing students more choices, and that
subsequently student participation will be observed during one or more discussions.

Reflection 3.3

Write a research question for an observational study that you would really like to do.

Plan: Setting and Participants

Before beginning your action research study, it is very important to carefully define your participants, the location of the study, and the time in which it will occur before beginning. This is sometimes referred to as the problem space, i.e. the time and space boundaries that delineate your observations. For example, your research question could be: "How well are students engaged with the learning center on ramps?" Your problem space could be defined as observing a classroom of pre-kindergarten students during activity time from 9:30 until 10:15 daily over a three-week period. Carefully defining the participants, the time, and the place (and conscientiously following through with the observations) makes the study much more objective. If the problem space is not defined and observations are made haphazardly, there is a much greater chance that your attention will be drawn to the center when either something very positive or very negative happens, for instance, pre-school students successfully complete their construction of a ramp and shout excitedly. Since your observation was not continuous and systematic, the nuances of student behavior during other parts of the activity may be lost, and it is likely that your conclusions will be skewed in an overly positive or negative direction.

The elements of the problem space written into the *Setting and Participants* sections of the research report is similar to the one described in Chapter 2 on interviews. The individual participants should be described with some detail. These details should all be relevant to the research question. For instance, if you are researching students who are proficient in math, you should indicate age, gender, and the reason why you selected these students as highly capable, such as grades, test scores, classroom observations, homework assignments, or some other criteria.

Reflection 3.4

(a) Use the research question you created in Reflection 3.3 as a basis for describing a hypothetical problem space, including the times and place of the observations.

_____

_____

_____

_____

(b) For the same research questions, describe the participants. Include their grade and ability levels, ethnicity, gender, special needs, and any other relevant information. Provide a reason for including them in the study, such as how their participation addresses the research question.

_____

_____

_____

_____

Collect Data

When making observations, data can be collected in a variety of ways, including audio or video recording, journaling, or notetaking. Audio or videotaping has the advantage of preserving all the information so it can be examined repeatedly. No equipment is required for notetaking and journaling. However, taking notes is only viable if you are not teaching at the time of the observations. If you were teaching, then journaling would enable you to record your observations as soon as you finished your teaching. The sooner you record your observations after teaching, the more details you are likely to capture.

Reflection 3.5

What type of data collection would be most effective for the research question you created in Reflection 3.3?

_____

_____

_____

_____

Bracketing

Bracketing is a technique used when making observations. It involves thoroughly examining your previous thoughts and experiences regarding the subject of your observations (Van Manen, 1990). Try to identify your assumptions and prejudices, then put them in "brackets" while you observe. In other words temporarily suspend your biases, so that you can make impartial and objective observations. When observing, the researcher should be as open as possible to anything and everything going on around her. Examine the setting thoroughly including what is on the walls, how the room is arranged, and what messages are communicated to children. Watch closely how participants enter the setting, how they engage with each other, and how engaged they are with the lesson. You must watch attentively, seeing the world (the problem space) with new eyes, because the most valuable insights can rarely be predicted. Researchers often refer to this approach as "making the familiar strange."

You should be meticulous and thorough. Take careful notes or record your observations with a cassette or video camera. You will need time to reflect on what you have seen, so it is important not to rule out some potentially significant data by jumping to conclusions too quickly. Withholding judgment as long as possible provides time for new insights to bubble to the surface. Taking this approach will lead to more objective observations.

Reflection 3.6

You can practice by trying to be as systematic and thorough as possible as you observe your immediate surroundings. Look around you and carefully examine your environment for the next 5-10 minutes. What do you notice that you hadn't noticed previously?

_____

_____

_____

_____

_____

Collect Data: Observe from Different Perspectives

As part of a systematic approach, you should try to consciously make observations from different perspectives. Deliberately assuming alternative perspectives can yield more insight on the subject and provide a broader basis for making interpretations. For purposes of illustration and to gain some practice with shifting your perspectives, carefully examine the journal entry in Box 3.1. These observations were recorded by a seventh grade social studies teacher after finishing a short unit in which she introduced cooperative learning as a teaching strategy. Carefully read her observations and interpret them from a management, motivation, and thinking skills perspectives.

BOX 3.1 JOURNAL ENTRY

Purpose

The purpose of these observations was to determine the effectiveness of cooperative learning groups. The unit learning goals were for students to understand the strategic advantages for both North and South, the overall strategy for each side, and the resulting outcomes of these strategic approaches.

Participants and Setting

This observation was conducted in a seventh grade social studies class. In this class, there are 20 students, 12 boys and 8 girls. Of these, 14 are Caucasian, 3 are Hispanic, and 3 are African-American. Two of these students are receiving instruction in English as a second language. Five students have IEPs (Individualized Learning Plans), and three students are receiving medication for ADHD. There is one special needs student who receives help from the resource teacher. This student is a girl with very low reading comprehension and writing ability. The class as a whole is below grade level in reading and math. Three of them are below the 20th percentile in both subject areas. However, there are two students who are released from class to participate in the gifted and talented program. These two students have extremely high ability in reading comprehension, writing ability, and their ability to reason and problem solve.

Data Collection: Observations

To accomplish these goals, the students were organized into five cooperative learning groups of four students each. In each group, three of the four students were assigned individual roles. There was a facilitator, a recorder, and a reporter. The facilitator's role in each group was to lead the discussion and activity of the group. The groups were instructed to use the Internet, reading materials, and other resources to compile a list of strategies and strategic advantages for each side. Then each group had to address these questions and provide supporting evidence for their answers:

1 Which side had the best strategy?
2 Which side had the most advantages?
3 Which side made the best use of their resources?
4 How could each side have changed the outcomes of the war by changing their strategy?

The recorder recorded the group's answers, and the reporter's role was to report the group's findings to the rest of the class.

Analysis

Three of the five groups compiled a list of strategic advantages within the first class period. They talked in a low tone, made lots of eye contact, and gave direction to the recorders as they were writing. Two of the groups were louder, with frequent bursts of laughter. The recorder seemed to be writing at a much slower pace. In one group, two of the students talked and laughed with each other, while two of the other group members talked more quietly and referred to the materials. In the other group, two students left their seats to go look out the window. Both groups had to be reminded to be quieter.

When I approached these two groups I could see their list of strategic advantages was incomplete. They were having difficulty using the resources to find the information they needed. When I asked them if they needed help, the two ELL students said they didn't understand the assignment. Lacking a factual foundation, both groups had difficulty answering the four higher level questions on the assignment. Their answers appeared to be unsupported opinion. Only one or two of the group members of this group contributed to the ensuing whole class discussion.

The other three groups were more successful in creating a complete list of strategic advantages for both sides. They were split on which side had the best strategy. Two of those groups favored the North's strategic advantages, while one group favored the South. One student said, "With their advantage in population and industry, only the incompetence of the generals could have kept the North from winning the war." Defending the opposite point of view, another student said, "Even with the North's advantages in soldiers and supplies, the South did not have

(Continued)

(Continued)

to win. They only had to avoid losing, and they nearly did it." However, only one of the four groups that got their list together could suggest plausible strategies for altering the outcomes of the Civil War. The plans for the other two groups were not consistent with the historical facts, and the students failed to provide a very convincing rationale to support their strategies.

At the end of the class period, there was a whole class discussion of the strategic advantages for both sides during the Civil War. About half of the class participated in the discussion. Regarding the question as to which side had the most resources and best strategy, many students were able to provide informed opinions and support them with factual information. There were fewer responses to the question regarding which side made the best use of their resources. However, Elise and Justine, both gifted students, argued passionately and credibly that the North's strategic use of resources would have eventually overcome any Southern military strategy.

During the discussion, there was some talking among students at inappropriate times. Some of the students had to be reminded to stop talking frequently. Three students were not able to keep their focus on the front of the room. Their attention wandered, and when called on, these students were not able to answer questions.

Analysis: Making Comparisons

One way to shift your perspective while observing is to create some kind of comparison. Sometimes, the contrast among participants or situations can be informative. For example, you could compare observations made at different times, in different locations, or with different participants.

Reflection 3.7

In the example above, compare the differences in observations between the three groups that were on task, and the two groups that were off task.

_____

_____

_____

_____

_____

Analysis: Changing Conceptual Frames

A second approach would be to make observations through different conceptual lenses, for example, viewing student behavior from the perspective of management issues, motivational concerns, or levels of student thinking skills.

Reflection 3.8

If your emphasis was on management and motivation, what observations above would you be most likely to notice?

_____

_____

_____

_____

To view students for the purpose of identifying their level of thinking, teachers may draw on a variety of descriptions (e.g., Schiever, 1991; Beyer, 1997), which may include descriptions of how students apply, analyze and synthesize ideas; make generalizations; draw conclusions; or compare and contrast ideas. One of the most familiar is Bloom's taxonomy, which describes six levels of thinking, including knowledge, comprehension, application, analysis, synthesis, and evaluation. The knowledge level is the lowest level of Bloom's taxonomy, and each of the five succeeding levels of the taxonomy represents an additional layer of complexity in thinking. Below is a brief summary of Bloom's taxonomy of educational objectives (for a more detailed description, see Further Reading on p. 200).

1   Knowledge: students recall, remember, or recognize previously learned information.
2   Comprehension: students demonstrate their understanding of ideas or relationships.
3   Application: students apply what they have learned in a new setting.
4   Analysis: students break down ideas into their component parts to promote deeper understanding.
5   Synthesis: students create new ideas by integrating ideas into larger patterns.
6   Evaluation: students express an opinion or a value judgment and justify it.

Reflection 3.9

If you used Bloom's taxonomy as a conceptual frame, which of the observations in Reflection 3.7 would be the most relevant?

_____

_____

_____

_____

_____

_____

_____

Analysis: Combining and Recombining Perspectives

A third approach for observing students is to integrate observations from perspectives into different combinations.

Reflection 3.10

What observations could be made about the motivation of the on task groups and thinking skills of the off task groups? What insight do you gain by combining these different perspectives?

_____

_____

_____

_____

_____

Reflection: Interpretations

In the preceding sections, you examined a teacher's journal entry of a unit on cooperative learning from a variety of perspectives. Carefully review your observations, then provide an interpretation of them in Reflection 3.11.

Reflection 3.11

Your interpretation will be an explanation of why the students responded to the lesson as they did. You are not limited to one interpretation. In fact, it is desirable to generate as many competing interpretations as possible. Even an unlikely interpretation may become more plausible with the accumulation of more data.

_____

_____

_____

_____

_____

_____

Reflection: Develop New Teaching Strategies

Observations are often very suggestive of new teaching strategies.

Reflection 3.12

Use your understanding of the teaching episode above to generate new teaching strategies. If needed, consult outside sources, such as educational journals or the internet for more ideas. Suggest other ways you could find new teaching strategies.

_____

_____

_____

_____

Reflection: Justification

Using the observational data given above, provide a rationale for the teaching strategies you have suggested in Reflection 3.12. Justification is important because it provides the link between your data, best practice, research-based strategies, and educational theory.

Reflection 3.13

Give as many supporting reasons for using your strategies as possible.

_____

_____

_____

_____

_____

_____

_____

_____

---

5 Using Checklists

The previous section addressed more open-ended observations of students, i.e., observations made without a preconceived idea of student behaviors. You can also create your own checklist in order to target other student behaviors in which you are more interested. Costa and Garmston (2002) have compiled a list of student behaviors in which teachers are interested and will often request feedback. Any of these behaviors can be observed for the amount of time one or more students engaged in them, the number of times students engaged in them, or through a written description of what occurs related to the designated behavior. A sample checklist of ten student behaviors is shown in Table 3.1.

TABLE 3.1 Checklist of sample student behaviors

Student Behavior	Description	No. of Tallies	Time (min.)
1 Volunteering responses			
2 On-task student-to-student interactions			
3 Requesting assistance			
4 Off task student-to-student interaction			
5 Interrupting, interfering			
6 Name calling, put downs, inappropriate language			
7 Distractability			
8 Using correct terminology			
9 Applying rules, algorithms, procedures, formulas			
10 Supplying supportive details, rationale, examples			

Some additional student behaviors compiled by Costa and Garmston include:

1   Attentiveness (on task, volunteering, note taking).
2   Preparedness (participation, sharing, homework, materials).
3   Managing materials (AV equipment, textbooks, library books, supplies).
4   Language patterns (syntax, grammar, spelling, punctuation).
5   Learning styles (verbal, auditory, kinesthetic, cognitive styles, tolerance for ambiguity, friendships).

Reflection 3.14

Create a checklist for your classroom by filling in numbers 1–10 in Table 3.2 below. Choose behaviors that are most appropriate for you. You can draw from the Flanders Interactional Analysis (Flanders, 1970), from Costa and Garmston, or use other student behaviors in which you are interested.

---

6 Analyzing Student Work

Making observations about student work is another useful source of action research data for diagnosing problems with learning and developing new teaching strategies. Student products that reflect long-term changes in student thinking or skill development are especially useful, such as student writing, art work, or musical performances. These types of student products are complex, and their assessment could benefit from sustained reflection. During such an inquiry, observations of student work should not be limited to the criteria specified on a rubric. The work in question should be observed without preconception in the systematic and careful manner described earlier.

One approach to using student work is to compare the work of students at different levels of ability. Using this approach requires choosing two representative students whose work is examined in depth. For example, one of the selected students could represent high achieving students and the other could represent low achieving students, as

TABLE 3.2 Checklist of self-selected student behaviors

Student Behavior	Description	No. of Tallies	Time (min.)
1 _____			
2 _____			
3 _____			
4 _____			
5 _____			
6 _____			
7 _____			
8 _____			
9 _____			
10 _____			

determined by standardized achievement test scores. Here is a seventh grader's response to the question, is there life on other planets?

> I do think there is life on other planets in the univers, but meby not on any in this galaxy. Otherwise it is pointless for the planets to even be there. Somewhere in the universe there has to be a planet that is as close to it's sun as the earth is to it is to the sun. If we can live on this planet, then there must be something like it with other life forms on it too. They may be very similar to us, or very different, depending on how they have adapted. We can't be the only ones in the solar system. For all we know, our parents could be aliens.

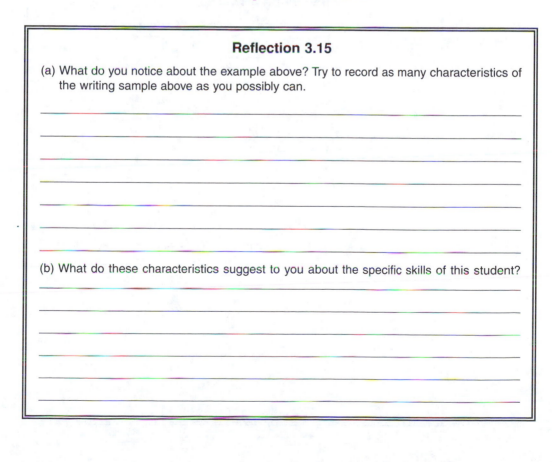

Reflection 3.15

(a) What do you notice about the example above? Try to record as many characteristics of the writing sample above as you possibly can.

_____

_____

_____

_____

_____

_____

(b) What do these characteristics suggest to you about the specific skills of this student?

_____

_____

_____

_____

_____

Here is another seventh grader's response to the same prompt asking if he believed there was life on other planets:

It is possible there might be different lifeforms on other planets in the universe. There is just about an unlimited number of possibilities of where a different type of lifeform would exist. For example, the planet Venus may support some type of life due to the atmosphere. The beings could possibly be acid type because of the toxic atmosphere on Venus.

But I don't really think that their are other places with life besides earth. There are four main features that a planet would need to support human life. It would need a biosphere, lithosphere, a hydroshere, and an atmosphere. If the planet didn't have one of those features the other features wouldn't function properly.

Most planets we know would not be able to support life because they don't have all of these elements. Without a hydrosphere, humans would die. Without water humans can die. Oxygen is important because without oxygen humans die right away. The planet would need to be close to the sun. The reason it needs to be close to the sun is because the sun provides solar energy and warmth which human beings need. The planet would have to rotate on an axis. If the planet didn't rotate one side of the planet would be dark all of the time and humans wouldn't be able to find food because the plants couldn't survive. If the plants couldn't survive, the animals couldn't survive, and the animals couldn't get any food from the animals. If there, is life in the universe, it is really good at hiding, because there has been nothing big to suggest that life exists.

Reflection 3.16

(a) What similarities and differences do you notice between the two examples given above? Make a list of factual observations below.

_____

_____

_____

_____

_____

_____

_____

_____

(b) What do these differences suggest to you about the specific abilities of each student?

_____

_____

_____

_____

_____

_____

_____

Reflection: Develop New Teaching Strategies

After the classroom work of each student is systematically observed and interpreted, new strategies are developed based on that analysis. Examining the work of only two students allows time to think more deeply about the learning of individual students, thus enabling the development of more effective strategies. In addition, once the strategies have been developed for an individual student, they can be used with the rest of the class. Analyzing students of differing abilities will result in strategies that can be applied in both the high and low ends of the class.

Reflection 3.17

How did comparing the two examples above enhance your analysis? Take a moment to reflect, and then write down your thoughts below.

_____

_____

_____

---

7 Analyzing Student Talk

Analyzing student talking can provide even more specific observations of student performance and thus serve as another important means for generating new teaching strategies. In the following sections, student talking will be examined from three different perspectives: (1) the amount of content knowledge revealed in student talk; (2) the student's ability to elaborate when responding to open-ended questions; and (3) the quality of student-to-student interactions.

Content Knowledge

Evaluating student talk for the acquisition of content knowledge is very similar to assessing student writing, especially if a transcript of student talk is available for analysis. To get a sense of the possibilities for analyzing content knowledge through student talk, read through the transcript excerpts below. The first was taken from near the beginning of a unit on surface area and volume. The students are trying to explain why ice cream containers are packaged in different shapes. The second was taken two weeks later near the end of the unit. Take note of the differences in vocabulary and content knowledge embedded in the students' responses.

Transcript 1

Teacher:	Okay! A lot of you already have some good ideas, so all I want you to do is share your ideas with each other, okay? Share your ideas with each other. Remember that I would like to (inaudible) contributing today. And some of you I've already heard, almost all of you, I didn't talk to each and every one have some idea of why things are shaped ... are the way they are as far as ice cream containers, so who feels they want to start? Who feels like ... Carl, go ahead.
Carl:	I think they have different containers to fit people's needs because like that one on the end behind, that's, like, for a person who wants some ice cream on their own and they, like, have that. And, like, the gallon, whatever in the box, rectangular prism size is for bigger families or whatever and it's just, like ... yeah ... different people's needs.
Teacher:	So, multiple packages to fit different needs. All right, Chuck, go ahead.
Chuck:	Well, those, um ... like, the cylinder boxes and those others um ... those are used a lot by Haagen-Das, and Ben & Jerry's, and Blue Bunny and those are really big and well known companies, but like you'll see Hy-Vee ice cream in the square ones and think the little ... well, those aren't square ... the rectangular prism boxes are a little cheaper than just the hard ones. But the circular, well, some of these, are easier to use because there's no corners for the ice cream to get stuck on.
Teacher:	Oh! I've never thought of the corner things.

In contrast, compare the talk in Transcript 1 to Transcript 2, which was taken from the last discussion during the unit. In the excerpt below, the students are explaining the features of a package designed to hold ping pong balls, which they have designed and constructed the package as part of a project. What differences do you see between the student talk in the first and second excerpt?

Transcript 2

Teacher:	Okay. Who did I say next? Chuck? Ah, Chuck!
Chuck:	Okay, this is my smallest cube. I just made cubes because cubes have small surface areas for their volume so I was worried about cost a lot.
Teacher:	Okay.
Chuck:	Trying to have a low cost. So then this one holds eight ping pong balls. It costs $3.47. It's 7.6 centimeters by 7.6 centimeters. Its surface area is 346 square centimeters. And the volume is 438.976 cubic centimeters.
Teacher:	All right. What questions do you have for Chuck? Okay, Steve?
Steve:	Why did he choose a box and not like a prism?
Chuck:	I chose a cube because they have a really small surface area. Because we were working with the real cube—centimeter cubes and then whenever all the dimension were all close together then it had the smallest surface area so I did cubes so then it would cost less.
Teacher:	All right. All right. Thanks. Anything else? Um ... anyone else have a question for Chuck?

Reflection 3.18

What differences in vocabulary and content knowledge do you notice between the two transcripts? List as many observations as possible below.

_____

_____

_____

_____

_____

_____

Elaboration

Elaboration refers to the students' ability to fully articulate their ideas. Their ability to speak at length on a subject provides an initial indication that they are knowledgeable about a topic, and in addition, it provides an opportunity for teachers to listen for more sophisticated student thinking skills. Without extensive student talking, further and more thorough assessment is not possible. The research on classroom interactions has consistently shown that even in classes with a high level of student participation, teachers talk twice as much as students.

To precisely calculate student elaboration requires making a transcript of teacher and student dialogue, probably from an audio or videotaping. With a transcript, you simply count the number of words spoken by the teacher and the total number of words spoken by the student. Then calculate the number of teacher words per speaking turn by dividing the total number of words spoken by the teacher by the total number of turns. This yields the average number of words spoken per turn. As an illustration, examine the following excerpt taken from a discussion in a seventh grade mathematics class on calculating surface area:

Teacher:	... little ways, yes, okay? Is that what? And this, and this would be divided up four ways. Okay? So, Justin were you able to get this one? How did you do it?
Justin:	Well, what I did was, I took the eighteen inch height and, like … like … well, like I divided it up into four and stuff and ...
Teacher:	So, did you divide it up like your paper sort of in your mind or on your paper?
Justin:	In my mind. And then (inaudible) that face of it I got fifty-four or just that surface area of that face ...
Teacher:	Are you talking, which face are you talking about?
Justin:	The one that you have
Teacher:	This was fifty ...
Justin:	four.
Teacher:	Okay. Let's check that out. You have eighteen by four. So we're going to take eighteen times four. Eighteen times … does that make sense to you, Justin, or did when you divided it up, you could count it? I don't think this

is in eighteen parts. Not even close, okay? We'd have to go a lot more than that. So, we're going to do a grid of eighteen by four.

Justin: That's seventy-two.

Teacher: Yeah, you've got it. Seventy-two squares.

Reflection 3.19

1   First count the number of teacher turns._____

2   Then count the total number of words spoken by the teacher._____

3   Then compute the average number of words spoken per turn._____

4   Then count the number of student turns._____

5   Then count the total number of words spoken by the student._____

6   Then compute the average number of words spoken per turn by the student._____

7   Then compute the ratio of teacher to student words._____

Let's try another example from the same seventh grade mathematics class. In this discussion, the students are using their understanding of surface area and volume to compare the relative merits of packages designed for marketing ping pong balls. Make a few informal observations about the differences in this transcript from the previous one as you read through the excerpt below. Then, take a few moments to calculate the ratio between teacher and student talk.

Teacher: Okay. Give Nathan your attention and respect.

Nathan: Usually you get your ping pong rackets with the ... with your tables and even if you wanted to play doubles, you could get more but if—they'd be different rackets, so it'd be like "oh, this is different that's why you're winning" or something so people could get into an argument or something. But also you could make this—ah, you could make this bigger if you had the same dimensions ...

Teacher: Wait, wait, wait. Make sure you're giving Nathan your attention and respect. Go ahead.

Nathan: If you had the same dimensions, you could make it just as big. Like if I had my diameter the same as maybe her height and then I had my height the same as her, whatever, it would be just more cost efficient. And I know that when you have the balls and you put them together in four, the diameter's going to increase due to the—'cuz the—like—should I draw it on the board or something?

Teacher: Just explain.

Nathan: Cuz if you have four, it's going to increase because you can't put those things together but that's only going to make it increase by maybe two centimeters and that's not going to add too much—that's not going to add too much surface area—er, volume, so it would still be more cost efficient. But a suh-phere I think would be the most cost efficient. I think we all—or I think we all had this. I think the best design would be a suh-phere. And you could package it, like, you could hold it in a ball and, like, have little shelves just, like, holding it.

Teacher: A sphere would actually be the most cost effective. That is the least surface area. This is what I need you to do.

Sharon: Can I say something real quick?

Teacher: Very quickly, Sharon.

Sharon: Okay, I know that you guys are debating about Allan's, we're all like going for Larry's a bunch of us. And one thing is what if you might want—what if you want to play doubles but it's not going to be, like, we're not worrying about everybody arguing who's a better—who's got a better paddle. I mean, different brands would still say, like, oh yeah, that one's better. And then you could pick her big pack to put on the shelves and his small one to put on the shelves and then you'd get people ...

Teacher: So you could get both of them.

Reflection 3.20

1   First count the number of teacher turns._____

2   Then count the total number of words spoken by the teacher._____

3   Then compute the average number of words spoken per turn._____

4   Then count the number of student turns._____

5   Then count the total number of words spoken by the student._____

6   Then compute the average number of words spoken per turn by the student._____

7   Then compute the ratio of teacher to student words._____

Reflection 3.21

(a) Summarize your observations from the two examples above in the space below. What similarities or differences do you notice between these two examples?

_____

_____

_____

_____

_____

_____

_____

(Continued)

(Continued)

(b) How do you interpret the differences between the two examples?

_____

_____

_____

_____

_____

_____

Reflection 3.22

What kinds of strategies would encourage more student elaboration? Consider wait time, asking more open-ended questions, asking probing questions, and giving preparation time in small groups. You may also want to use those as search terms in order to find more specific strategies.

_____

_____

_____

Reflection 3.23

Use your knowledge of research-based instructional strategies and your experience to justify the strategies above.

_____

_____

_____

_____

Charting Student Response Patterns

By charting their students' response patterns, teachers can determine how equally participation is spread through the class. An equal distribution of participation encourages student engagement. However, previous research has shown that teachers can favor some students over others based on ability, gender, ethnicity, and their location in the classroom (Patchen, 2006; Sadker & Sadker, 1985; Sauer, Popp, & Isaacs, 1984). Charting student response patterns is a relatively simple way to ensure a more equal distribution

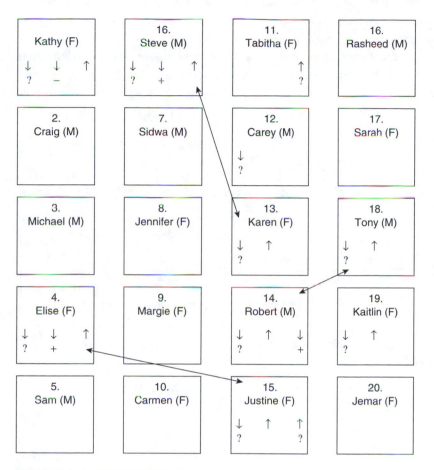

FIGURE 3.3 Observation chart

of participation. Such an analysis could provide a useful indication of participation patterns on a class, subgroup and individual basis.

There are several ways that participation could be recorded. A colleague could be invited to tally student responses, or the class could be videotaped and the response pattern charted from the videotape. Simpler yet, use a seating chart, design a participation chart, or create some other type of chart with a list of students' names and keep track of student participation during the discussion. This approach doesn't require any equipment and offers the added advantage of serving as an accountability strategy. Students who are aware the teacher is recording their participation are often more likely to contribute to the discussion (Dallimore, Hertenstein, & Platt, 2004). The type of student-to-student interactions can provide an indication of students' dispositions towards discussion, their ability to facilitate talk, their ability to listen and evaluate ideas, and their ability to synthesize the comments of their classmates.

Look at the observation chart (Figure 3.3). The arrow indicates the direction of the interaction. An arrow pointing downward indicates the teacher is addressing the student, and, pointing upward, it indicates the student is addressing the teacher. A downward pointing arrow with a question mark indicates the teacher is asking a question. A plus sign indicates praise and a minus sign indicates the teacher rejected the student answer as incorrect. An upward pointing arrow indicated the student answered a question: when accompanied by a question mark, it indicates the student asked a question. Arrows pointing between students indicates that students addressed each other, either in agreement or disagreement, to elaborate on a previous response, or to ask a question.

Reflection 3.24

(a) Based on your examination of the participation chart, make as many factual observations as you are able.

_____

_____

_____

_____

(b) If you knew that Elise and Justine were high ability students, what insight would that add to your observations?

_____

_____

_____

_____

(c) If you knew that Jemar, Carmen, and Rasheed were African-Americans, and Kaitlin, Justine, and Michael were Latino students, what insight would that add to your observations?

_____

_____

_____

_____

(d) What are you able to infer about the interactions in this classroom based on your observations?

_____

_____

_____

_____

_____

Reflection 3.25

What kinds of strategies would encourage more student-to-student interaction? Consider teaching students to ask higher-level questions, to employ effective listening skills and to respond to their classmate's comments, and to use verbal and nonverbal cues to encourage the participation of other students. You may want to use those as search terms in order to find more specific strategies.

_____

_____

_____

_____

_____

Reflection 3.26

Use your knowledge of research-based instructional strategies and your experience to justify the strategies above.

_____

_____

_____

_____

_____

_____

8 Summary

This chapter showed you how to make observations about students, their work, and their talk. Direct and systematic observations of student behaviors provide an opportunity for an open-ended investigation of student learning. This has the advantage of discovering difficulties with learning in a timely fashion, thus enabling the rapid development of new teaching strategies. Observations of student work can provide insight into the development of student thinking and serve as a vehicle for suggesting new strategies to enhance student thinking. Finally, an analysis of student talking can provide insight into the content knowledge of students, the students' ability to elaborate, and the quality of student-to-student interactions. In general, observational data can serve as a useful tool for developing new teaching strategies.

four
Observing Teachers

Being a teacher researcher has become for me an instrument for reflection and change. It has allowed for both renewal and growth in my personal life and my professional life, and what I have learned will continue to nurture my teaching in the future.

(Nancy Hubbard, 1996, p. 116)

1 Introduction

The aim of this chapter is to introduce several methods for observing teachers. Some of these methods lend themselves to self-observation through journaling, audiotaping, or videotaping. Other methods involve collaborating with another teacher or action researcher in the observation. Using the second approach could involve an open-ended observation, during which the observer systematically records classroom observations in his or her notes. Or it could involve more structured observations based on a checklist on which an observer would record the frequency of a set of pre-specified behaviors.

Making systematic observations of your teaching provides an opportunity to determine whether or not your teaching is aligned with best practices. Open-ended observations can enhance your awareness of areas where improvement is needed. More targeted observations provide specific feedback regarding whether or not your teaching is aligned with practices that promote student involvement and achievement.

The limitations of observing teaching are related to data collection, especially when you desire to make observations about your own teaching. Observing yourself may require collecting data with the use of specialized equipment, like a video camera or a tape recorder. Or you may have to work with another person who can keep a running record of how often you perform specific behaviors. Working collaboratively could be a very positive approach for two teachers who can find the time to observe each other's classrooms.

The previous chapter began discussing open-ended observations of students and their work, and then moved to investigations of more targeted behaviors related to specific patterns of student talking. Similarly, this chapter will begin with more open-ended observations of teachers, and then move to more specific and targeted verbal behaviors. Examples of open-ended approaches to observing teachers could include journaling or viewing videotapes of your teaching. Examples of the more structured approaches would include using checklists for identifying specific teaching behaviors or using audio or videotapes for the purpose of analyzing your question asking strategies or other types of verbal behaviors. In both cases, the purpose of the analysis is to identify specific verbal behaviors associated with improved student thinking and learning.

2 Steps in Observing Teachers

As is the case with all forms of action research, you will need a plan for collecting your observational data. The following are some suggested steps:

1   Plan
    (a) Establish the goals of the project. State your goals in the form of a research question. What is it that you want to learn?
    (b) Determine the context of the observation—what class, what topic, and when?
    (c) Decide on data collection method.
2   Collect data
    (a) Collect your data either by audio or videotaping, a verbatim transcript, or a checklist.
3   Analyze
    (a) As you conduct the observation, withhold judgment. Record factual information. Try to avoid making inferences or imposing your judgment on the data.
4   Reflect
    (a) Interpret the data.
    (b) Develop new strategies.
    (c) Justify your strategies.
    (d) Write a summary report.

3 Open-Ended Observations

The most open-ended approach to observing your teaching is simply to record a teaching episode, either through an audio or videotape, then examine the recording for the purpose of making improvements. This approach can help you attend to previously unexamined aspects of your teaching. After you have recorded your teaching on audio or videotape, follow the same process of describing, interpreting, developing and justifying new strategies that is prescribed throughout this book.

Reflection 4.1

Plan: Expectations Start the process by describing how you prepared for the lesson and what you expected to happen.

_____

_____

_____

_____

Collect Data Record your observations of what actually happened.

_____

_____

_____

_____

Reflections: Interpretations Explain what happened and why you think it happened.

_____

_____

_____

Reflections: Develop New Teaching Strategies What strategies would lead to improvements in your teaching? Where could you look for new strategies? What kind of professional growth activities would be appropriate?

_____

_____

_____

_____

---

4 Using Checklists

Observations of teachers can also target specific, predetermined behaviors. In this type of observation, an observer will use a checklist to record the frequency of the specified behaviors. The checklist will consist of a list of particular behaviors on a data coding sheet. There are numerous checklists to fit a wide variety of purposes (see Further Reading on p. 200). If you find you like this methodology, you may want to search the literature for checklists that have been used in the past.

For the purposes of illustration, we will demonstrate the use of the Flanders' Interaction Analysis (Flanders, 1970). The Flanders Interaction Analysis is one of the most widely known checklists and is specifically designed for investigating the quality of teacher and student verbal interactions. In the following sections, you will be led through an activity with a modified version of the Flanders Interaction Analysis. As part of his coding system, Flanders divided classroom interactions into 10 categories (Box 4.1).

BOX 4.1 CATEGORIES FOR ANALYSIS OF TEACHER INTERACTION

1   *Accepts Students' Feelings*: Accepts and clarifies the feeling tone of the students in a non-threatening manner. Feelings may be positive or negative.

2   *Gives Praise to Students*: Praises or encourages students' action or behavior. Acknowledges students with a nod or other reassuring gesture.

3   *Responds to Student Query, Idea or Statement*: Clarifying, building, or developing ideas or suggestions by a student. As the teacher brings more of his/her own ideas into the conversation, a shift is made to category five below.

4   *Questions*: Asking a question about content or procedure with the intent that a student answers. There are three types of questions that can be asked. They are:

   – Level I: Simple response
   – Level II: Critical thinking
   – Rhetorical: No student answer is expected.

5   *Lecturing*: Giving facts or opinions about content or procedures.

6   *Giving Directions*: Directions, commands, or orders, with which a student is expected to comply.

7   *Criticizing Student Behavior*: Statements intended to change student behavior from non-accepting to acceptable.

8   *Student Responds to Teacher Idea or Question*: Talk by students in response to the teacher. Teacher initiates the contact or solicits students' statements.

9   *Student-Initiated Talk*: Talk by students, which they initiate.

10 *Silence or Confusion*: Pauses, short periods of silence, and periods of confusion in which communication cannot be understood by the observer.

The categories above are also summarized in the Interaction Data Analysis in Table 4.1. To complete the following activity, you will use this table to record your observations as you watch a 10-minute segment of videotaped teaching. You may want to either use a videotape of another teacher or videotape yourself teaching a 10-minute lesson. You may tape more minutes if wish, but 10 minutes is the very minimum required.

Coding the Observations

Before you begin coding interactions, you should be familiar with the categories of Interaction Analysis. You may also need to refer back to these pages as you analyze your data. Note that categories 1–4 describe *indirect teacher talk*, or teacher talk that fosters more student talk. Numbers 1–3 are responses to student comments. Categories 5–7 relate to *direct teacher talk*, such as lecturing or giving directions. Categories 8–10 refer to *student talk*. Of the 10 categories, 7 of them describe types of teacher talk and

TABLE 4.1 Flanders Interaction Analysis data table

Category	Tally Marks	No. of Tallies	% of Tallies
1 Accepts students' feelings			
2 Gives praise to students			
3 Responds to student query			
4 Question is asked			
5 Lecture			
6 Giving directions			
7 Criticize student behavior			
8 Student responds to teacher			
9 Student initiates the talk			
10 Silence or confusion			

only 3 describe types of student talk. This was consistent with Flanders' finding that even in very student-centered classrooms, two-thirds of the talking was done by the teacher. It was Flanders' contention that teachers who fostered more student talk in the classroom were generally more effective than those who relied exclusively on direct teacher talk.

As you watch the teaching video, use the tally sheet to record a tally mark every 10 seconds. (This is a modification of the Flanders system, which required a tally mark every 2 to 3 seconds.) In other words, once every 10 seconds you will make a tally on the interaction analysis table. The mark you make will be your interpretation of the nature of the classroom interaction as defined by Flanders' 10 categories. If you are observing a video of your own teaching, you may wish to analyze several lessons. One teaching segment will only give you feedback for that particular 10-minute lesson. More segments will give you a better overall understanding of your teaching style.

Reflection 4.2

How many total tally marks should you have if you were to use a 10-minute time frame?_____

Observations from Different Perspectives

After you have finished your observation, calculate the percentage of tallies for each category. The percentage is determined by dividing the number of tally marks for each category by the total number of tally marks, and then multiplying the decimal by 100. Because the column is named, you do not have to use a unit with your answer. This unit is understood. The percentage column should add up to 100%. Know that rounding up or down may cause your total percentage to vary, however.

Reflection 4.3

Does your percentage column add up to 100%, plus or minus a couple of percentage points? _____

By comparing a ratio of direct tally marks to the number of indirect tally marks, you can determine whether more direct or indirect teaching was used during this observation.

Determine the indirect to direct ratio by dividing the numerator and denominator each by the denominator. Your answer will be expressed as a *number to one*.

$$\frac{\text{Indirect tally mark total}}{\text{Direct tally mark total}} = \frac{\rule{3cm}{0pt}}{\rule{3cm}{0pt}} = \frac{\rule{3cm}{0pt}}{\rule{3cm}{0pt}}$$

Analyze the above mathematical statement. If you have a ratio greater than 1, then the type of talking during this observation was more *indirect*. If the ratio is less than 1, the type of talking during this observation was more *direct*. This means there was more emphasis on lecturing and giving of directions.

Based on the above ratio, did this teaching segment suggest you were utilizing more *indirect teacher communication or more direct teacher communication?* _____

Reflection 4.4

Summarize your observations by listing the percentages from Table 4.1 for each category below:

1 _____% Accepts Students' Feelings

2 _____% Gives Praise to Students

3 _____% Responds to Student Query, Idea or Statement

4 _____% Questions

5 _____% Lecturing

6 _____% Giving Directions

7 _____% Criticizing Student Behavior

8 _____% Student Responds to Teacher Idea or Question

9 _____% Student-Initiated Talk

10 _____% Silence or Confusion

Describe the overall pattern of teacher/student interactions.

_____

_____

_____

_____

What conclusions can you draw about the ratio of teacher to student talking in the classroom? As you reflect on the observations you made, keep these findings from Flanders' previous research in mind:

1   It is not unusual for teachers to do as much as 70% of the talking.
2   Student talk in the average classroom is about 24% of the total verbal behavior.
3   Teaching by lecturing, while often comprising 50% of the total interaction in the class, has been discovered in some classes to make up as little as 20% of the total verbal behavior.
4   Research shows a relationship between the extended use of student ideas by the teacher and pupil achievement.
5   The amount of praise used by the average teacher is between 1% and 2% of the total time spent in classroom interaction.

Reflections: Interpretations

As you study your teaching style or as you watch another teacher for a length of time, you may notice a teaching pattern emerge. While no one pattern should be considered better without considering the context of the interaction (the teacher purposes and the learning objectives), some patterns elicit more student interaction, and could be considered more effective when the teacher is trying to achieve particular learning outcomes. For example, Teacher A may ask a question (4) to get a narrow student response (8), and then may respond by asking another question (4). This is a 4-8-4 pattern as defined by the numbered categories in Table 4.1.

Reflection 4.5

Teacher B may approach the same question (4) in such a way as to invoke some student initiated talk (9), praise the student for a good answer (2), build on what was said (3), and initiate a new question (4). This is a 4-9-2-3-4 pattern. Consider these two situations. Which teacher (A or B) fostered more class participation in her classroom?

_____

_____

_____

_____

What kind of teaching strategies should Teacher A adopt to improve classroom interactions and increase student participation? Where could this teacher search for new strategies and what search terms would be appropriate?

_____

_____

_____

_____

_____

TABLE 4.2 Sample teacher behaviors

Teacher Behavior	Description	No. of Tallies	Time (min.)
1 Time getting class started			
2 Transitions			
3 Time spent with each group			
4 Monitoring seat work			
5 Interruptions			
6 Mannerisms (shifting weight, nodding)			
7 Body language, gestures, proximity			
8 Eye contact			
9 Accommodations (gifted, struggling, different cognitive styles)			
10 Adapting for language and culture			

The Flanders Interaction Analysis specifically targets verbal behaviors. You can also create your own checklist in order to target other teacher behaviors in which you are more interested. Costa and Garmston (2002) have compiled a list of behaviors on which teachers will often request feedback. Any of these behaviors can be observed for the amount of time a teacher engaged in them, the number of times a teacher engaged in them, or through a written description of what occurs related to the designated behavior. A sample checklist of ten teacher behaviors is shown in Table 4.2.

Some additional behaviors compiled by Costa and Garmston include:

1   Modality preference (visual, kinesthetic, and auditory modes of presentation).
2   Use of handouts (clarity, meaningfulness, adequacy, or complexity).
3   Use of audiovisual equipment.
4   Pacing.
5   Classroom arrangements (furniture placement, bulletin board space, multiple use of spaces).

Reflection 4.6

Create a checklist for your classroom by filling in numbers 1–10 in Table 4.3.

TABLE 4.3 Checklist of self-selected teacher behaviors

Teacher Behavior	Description	No. of Tallies	Time (min.)
1 _____			
2 _____			
3 _____			
4 _____			
5 _____			
6 _____			
7 _____			
8 _____			
9 _____			
10 _____			

(Continued)

(Continued)

Choose behaviors that are most appropriate for you. You can draw from the Flanders Interaction Analysis, from Costa and Garmston, or other teacher behaviors in which you are interested.

5 Analyzing Audiotapes, Videotapes, or Verbatim Transcripts

Observing teachers can also involve more specific investigations of their talking. Data is collected in this type of action research study by audiotaping, videotaping, or creating a verbatim transcript. Audio or videotaping provides an opportunity to repeatedly examine teacher talk during a specific teaching episode. Audio or videotapes can also be used to create a transcript of teacher talk. Transcripts provide another perspective and an opportunity to study the teacher's talk even more closely. If audio or videotape isn't available, an observer can create a verbatim transcript by selecting a brief, targeted segment of the class (e.g., 5 minutes) and recording teacher and student interactions word for word.

By recording the exact words of the teacher, a more detailed analysis of classroom interactions is possible. Typically, classroom interactions consist of a three-part cycle, which begins with a teacher question, is followed by a student response, and concludes with a follow-up comment by the teacher. This cycle of teacher and student interactions can be seen as relatively more and less open. Less open interactions would begin with a factual question, followed by a terse student response, and concluded with an evaluative comment by the teacher (e.g., "Correct."). More open interactions would begin with open-ended questions, followed by significant wait time, more elaborate student responses, and followed up with further probing questions or other teacher guidance of a less evaluative nature.

Each phase of this cycle can be analyzed, starting with teacher questions. Questions, which compose approximately 40% of all teacher talk, are often classified by educational taxonomies according to the objective they are intended to serve. One of the most widely known and used is Bloom's taxonomy (Bloom et al., 1956). In Box 4.2. a short definition and an example question is provided for each of the six levels of Bloom's taxonomy, beginning with the knowledge level.

BOX 4.2 THE SIX LEVELS OF BLOOM'S TAXONOMY

Knowledge Questions ask students to recall, remember, or recognize previously learned information.

Example: Who was the chief military strategist for the South during the Civil War?

Comprehension Questions ask students to demonstrate their understanding of ideas or relationships.
Example: How did Northern control of the Mississippi River contribute to their eventual victory?

Application Questions ask students to apply what they have learned in a new setting.
Example: How was the Battle of Gettysburg a result of the Southern strategy to win the war?

Analysis Questions ask students to break down ideas into their component parts to promote deeper understanding.
Example: Why did the North have a strategic advantage entering the Civil War?

Synthesis Questions ask students to integrate ideas into larger patterns.
Example: How could the South have won the war without foreign support?

Evaluation Questions ask students to express an opinion or a value judgment.
Example: Which side best used their strategic advantages in the Civil War, the North or the South?

The most critical distinction among questions is the difference between the knowledge level and higher levels on Bloom's taxonomy. Knowledge-level questions are often referred to as recall or recitation questions, and they are associated with a more teacher-directed, evaluative dialogue between teacher and student. The higher five levels of questions invite more student participation and encourage higher-level thinking skills. Therefore, it is especially important that you can distinguish between knowledge-level questions and higher-level questions.

Reflection 4.7

The following six questions are based on John Steinbeck's novel *Of Mice and Men*. Three are knowledge-level questions, and three are higher-level questions. Identify each of the following questions as either a knowledge-level question or as a question belonging to one of the other five levels of Bloom's taxonomy. Specify the exact name of the questions as either knowledge, evaluation, synthesis, analysis, application, or comprehension.

_____ 1 Where do the ranch hands usually go on Saturday night?

_____ 2 Do you think the death of Lenny was an appropriate way to end the novel? Explain why or why not.

_____ 3 Who were the two main characters in *Of Mice and Men?*

_____ 4 If you could change the ending of the novel, how would you do it?

_____ 5 In what state did the story take place?

_____ 6 How does the opening scene of the novel foreshadow the accidental killing of Curley's wife?

Teacher's Follow Up Moves

The teacher's follow-up moves are the comments teachers make after the student responds to a question. Identifying the teacher's follow up moves can also provide indications about the quality of teacher and student interactions. Most teachers make similar kinds of follow-up moves. (For more information on teacher follow-up moves, see Mercer (2000) in Further Reading.) Several examples of follow-up moves are described below.

- *Confirmations* A confirmation occurs when a teacher indicates the student has given the correct response to an elicitation. Examples of confirmation would include, "Right," "Good job," "I agree," "Okay," and "Good point."
- *Rejections* A rejection is when the teacher indicates to a student the answer is not correct. Examples of rejection would include: "No, try again," "Sorry, good guess," and "No, you need to think about that a little more." For the most part, teachers give far more confirmations than rejections in order to keep the flow of conversation moving.
- *Probing or Follow up Questions* Probing questions can also help students extend and improve the quality of their responses. Dantonio and Beisenherz (2001) divide questions into two categories. *Focus question* refers to a initial question the teacher uses to open up a topic or a subject for discussion. *Probing or follow-up questions* help students extend and improve the quality of their initial responses, e.g., "What do you mean by that?" or "Can you support your answer with examples?"
- *Cues* Most simply said, a cue is a clue. The teacher directs student attention towards a particular aspect of a question or problem for the purpose of guiding student responses.
- *Repetitions* A teacher repeats all or part of what a student says in order to confirm, emphasite, or question a student comment.
- *Reformulations* Teachers may also reformulate student responses. When teachers reformulate student comments, they restate what the student has said to better fit the teacher's purposes, e.g. to make it clearer, to introduce more formal language, or to make it more accessible to the rest of the class.
- *Elaborations* Teachers may also elaborate or add additional information to student responses. Teachers use elaborations to introduce new information or to help students make connections between seemingly unrelated ideas.

Reflection 4.7

The transcript excerpt below was taken from a fifth grade classroom. The class was discussing a chapter from the novel *Pinballs*. Each of the teacher's discourse moves in the transcript has been numbered. As you read through the transcript, use the list of terms given above to identify each of these discourse moves. Write your response in Reflection 4.8. After you have finished, discuss the following questions.

focus question	confirmation	reformulation	cue
probing question	rejection	repetition	elaboration

Teacher.   [1] What is the relationship between Kentucky Fried Chicken and child neglect in Harvey's life? What does it mean if you neglect something? If you have a pet and you are neglecting it, it means that you are not doing what?

Student: Taking good care of it.

Teacher: [2] You're not taking good care of it. [3] So what do you think child neglect is? Casey?

Student: Something that you, um ... remember from your childhood?

Teacher: [4] No, not really hon. Good guess though.

Student: Not taking good care of it.

Teacher: [5] Yeah, [6] not taking good care of a child. [7] That's what child neglect is. [8] So what is the connection between Kentucky Fried Chicken, child neglect, and Harvey? [9] Those three things kinda fit together in a triangle and what is it that makes those things fit together? Why are they all related? Elana, what did you say?

Student: Kentucky Fried Chicken was the light of Harvey's life because whenever his dad was late from work, Harvey would go get some Kentucky Fried Chicken and child neglect was related to Harvey's life because his father neglected him.

Teacher: [10] Yeah, [11] his father really didn't take good care of him. So when his father was late, it was easy for Harvey to go on over across the street to Kentucky Fried Chicken. So that's the way that they're connected. [12] Very good. What did you have?

1 _____

2 _____

3 _____

4 _____

5 _____

6 _____

7 _____

8 _____

9 _____

10 _____

11 _____

12 _____

Open and Closed Teacher/Student Interactions

Interactions between teachers and students can be more teacher directed or more student directed. More teacher-directed discourses will have some or all of the following characteristics.

1   a higher ratio of teacher-to-student talk;

2   a high proportion of knowledge-level or recall questions;

3   brief student responses;
4   evaluative teacher follow-up moves (confirmations or rejections);
5   little student-to-student interaction.

More open, student-centered interactions will have some or all of the following characteristics:

1   a higher ratio of student-to-teacher talk;
2   a high proportion of higher-level questions;
3   more elaborate student responses;
4   guided teacher follow-up moves, such as reformulations, probing questions, etc.;
5   increased student-to-student interaction.

The reason for comparing the two transcript excerpts below is to increase your awareness of the differences between more and less open classroom interactions. Both excerpts were taken from discussions in a seventh grade mathematics classroom during a unit on surface area and volume. The first excerpt is from a discussion that took place at the very beginning of the unit. The second excerpt is taken from a discussion that takes place near the midpoint of the same unit. Both of these discussions served important, albeit different, purposes within the unit, and this exercise is not meant to imply one discussion was better than the other. It is simply intended to help you become more aware of the differences between more open and closed interactions. In the spaces following the two excerpts, identify which of the two is more open, and provide a justification to support your choice.

In Chapter 3 we looked at the same except from the point of view of observing students, here study it with a view to considering the teacher-directed discourse.

Transcript 1

Teacher:	Okay! A lot of you already have some good ideas, so all I want you to do is share your ideas with each other, okay? Share your ideas with each other. Remember that I would like to (inaudible) contributing today. And some of you I've already heard, almost all of you, I didn't talk to each and every one, have some idea of why things are shaped ... are the way they are as far as ice cream containers, so who feels they want to start? Who feels like ... Carl, go ahead.
Carl:	I think they have different containers to fit people's needs because like that one on the end behind, that's, like, for a person who wants some ice cream on their own and they, like, have that. And, like, the gallon, whatever in the box, rectangular prism size is for bigger families or whatever and it's just, like ... yeah ... different people's needs.
Teacher:	So, multiple packages to fit different needs. All right, Chuck, go ahead.

Chuck:	Well, those, um ... like the cylinder boxes and those others um ... those are used a lot by Haagen-Das, and Ben & Jerry's, and Blue Bunny and those are really big and well known companies, but like you'll see Hy-Vee ice cream in the square ones and think the little ... well, those aren't square ... the rectangular prism boxes are a little cheaper than just the hard ones. But the circular, well, some of these, are easier to use because there's no corners for the ice cream to get stuck on.
Teacher:	Oh! I've never thought of the corner things.
Chuck:	Um ... we thought the freezer space ...
Teacher:	Wait. Make sure everybody's giving you their attention and respect ... go ahead.
Chuck:	The freezer space because some people have a freezer and some people have a smaller one. We thought that, the gallon one, you would want to bring home a gallon in a box, like a big, big box because gallons take a lot of room. And we thought the small one was made like that was because it's, like, if you want to buy ice cream like that, they make it more expensive because they don't sell it in that one, then they'd make more money off this one because if you had five people, you'd probably have to buy two or three of those things. One for each person maybe, or like one for every two persons and then and they're more expensive so that they people make more money than off the other two with discounts.

Transcript 2

Alisha:	Um, the surface area for that one is eighty-eight, but on one of the sides you're going to have to multiply twenty-four by two.
Teacher:	Um-hum—and that's ...
Alisha:	Forty-eight.
Teacher:	And then you have to multiply that by two.
Alisha:	Yeah!
Teacher:	Yeah, very good! Anybody else want to say it differently? Larry?
Larry:	Since this is the long one, it's not the longest one, but it's ...
Teacher:	The longest one would be one by one by forty-eight.
Larry:	Forty-eight. Yeah. This is longer than that and less cubed, cubicle or whatever, however ...
Teacher:	Less cubicle?
Larry:	Yeah.
Teacher:	I like that.
Larry:	However you say it. And so it's going to be longer so it's going to ... it's going to have more surface area.
Teacher:	Everybody okay with that? Is there any one that would be actually ... yes, this is bigger ... is there any one that would have a smaller surface than four by two by six? I want you to talk with your partner *only* about that. Is there any one that would be smaller than four by two by six? Remember last time, Larry just hinted at it, it's the one that's closest to a cube if you can get there. Closest to a cube.

Reflection 4.8

(a) What differences do you notice between the two transcripts? Record your factual observation in the spaces below.

_____

_____

_____

_____

_____

(b) What kind of strategies could be used to make the interactions above more open?

_____

_____

_____

_____

---

6 Summary

This chapter showed you how to make observations of teachers' interactions with students. The simplest approach is to record your teaching through audiotaping, videotaping, or journaling and to examine it. This approach enables open-ended observations, which means the researchers rely a great deal on their personal judgments as they interpret the data. More open-ended observations can increase your awareness of your teaching behaviors and perhaps suggest a more specific topic for investigation. A second approach is to target specific teacher behaviors as designated by a checklist of predetermined behaviors. This chapter used as an example one of the most well-known and widely used checklists, the Flanders Interaction Analysis. By tallying the number of observations in each category, researchers can begin to detect patterns from which broader inferences can be made about the teaching. A third approach to making observations is to analyze the specific use of language by teachers. Certain patterns of speech are considered more effective than others when trying to raise the level of discourse in the classroom, e.g., the use of higher level questions, increased wait time, and the increased use of guiding responses.

Part III
Gathering Perceptions

Part III consists of two chapters intended to show you how to conduct surveys and interviews. Surveys and interviews can be used to investigate the perceptions of students, teachers, or administrators on a variety of issues related to school. Examples would include how students are responding to a new instructional strategy, how teachers feel about implementing a new instructional strategy, or how parents feel about the school climate. Both are helpful at providing insights into what participants are thinking. Surveys, which are discussed in Chapter 5, can solicit more participants and thus provide a wider, more inclusive view of an issue. Interviews, which are discussed in Chapter 6, can probe more deeply into the thinking of individual participants, and thus add more depth and insight. When used together, surveys and interviews complement each other by providing both breadth and depth.

five
Using Surveys in Action Research

It is teachers who, in the end, will change the world of the school by understanding it.
(Lawrence Stenhouse, cited in Rudduck, 1988)

1 Introduction

Surveys are a very useful tool for the systematic gathering of perspectives, attitudes and self-reports of behavior. They can provide useful insights into the thoughts and opinions of your participants. Example studies would include surveying students about their reaction to an instructional innovation, teachers about the challenges of implementing a new reading program, and parents about their child's study habits.

Surveys offer the unique advantage of providing a window into the thinking of your participants. They also can provide insights beyond the scope of an interview study because they can reach more participants. Therefore, findings from a survey are usually representative of a larger group of people than interviews.

However, like all other forms of action research, surveys have their limitations. First, neither survey nor interview data can claim to represent the actual facts of the matter; they only represent the facts as the participants see them or choose to tell them. For instance, student responses to a reading interest survey may be influenced by their anger over a low grade or their eagerness to please the teacher. Second, surveys usually do not allow the same level of depth as interviews, nor do they lend themselves to follow-up questioning in the same way as interviews. That makes it doubly important to carefully consider your survey questions before asking them.

The aim of this chapter is to introduce readers to the specific techniques needed to conduct your own survey study. As readers read and respond to questions in the following sections, they will learn how to create a title for the survey, formulate a research question, select their participants, write survey questions, create a rating scale, pilot a survey, administer a survey, analyze the data, and draw conclusions. When you have finished this chapter, you will be ready to conduct an action research project using surveys.

2 Steps in Survey Research

As is the case with all forms of action research, you need a plan and must follow that plan from start to finish. The following are some suggested steps:

1   Plan
    (a) Establish the goals of the project. State your goals in the form of a research question. What is it that you want to learn?
    (b) Select your participants.
    – Do you want to restrict your survey to students in your classroom, in your school, or to a certain gender or ethnic background?
    – Do you want to include students in other schools?
    – What about parents and other teachers?
    (c) Create your survey. What will you ask and what type of response format will you use?
2   Collect data
    (a) Pilot the survey to make sure your respondents understand the questions and the response format, then make revisions based on feedback.
    (b) Administer the survey.
3   Analyze
    (a) Make objective observations about the survey data.
    (b) Analyze the survey data from different perspectives.
4   Reflect
    (a) Interpret.
    (b) Develop new teaching strategies.
    (c) Justify your strategies.
    (d) Write a summary report.

3 Plan

Topic Selection

Whether or not you choose to use a survey to gather data depends on your research question. There are many interesting questions for which teachers have an intuitive feel. But taking the extra time to collect data that would allow them to substantiate their "gut feelings" often does not occur. Using a survey method is a quick and easy way to gather data that may shed new light on old problems.

Before you begin thinking about specific research questions, spend a few minutes listing broad topic areas that would be of interest to most teachers in your school.

Reflection 5.1

Consider the eight general topics listed below. Once you have reviewed them, add 10–15 more topics to the list.

homework   extracurricular activities   lunchroom   academic rigor

bullying   school climate   cheating   drinking

_____

_____

_____

_____

_____

Research Question

Once you decide on a topic of interest, that topic must be written into a research question. Your research question should be direct and narrowly focused. Don't take on a topic that is so broad you will not be able to collect enough data to adequately answer the question. Some examples of survey research questions are:

■   What are parents' attitudes toward integrated mathematics in our school?
■   After attending one year of college, in what areas do our graduates feel our school best prepared them for college and in which areas did they feel least prepared?
■   How do student attitudes about science compare in elementary school, middle school and high school?

Reflection 5.2

(a) Student success in school, in many cases, seems to be closely tied to students' work habits at home. Write one research question whose answers would provide useful information to a teacher about homework habits.

_____

_____

_____

(b) Now write two more research questions about other education topics that are of interest to you.

Research Question 1 _____

_____

Research Question 2 _____

_____

Selecting Your Participants

Your research question will guide both your selection of participants and the questions you decide to ask them. Selecting your participants is a relatively simple process. Many times in school settings, your sample will consist of intact classes. For example, if your research question is about participation in extracurricular activities by middle school students, you would obviously want to administer the survey to all the students, if possible. This may present a challenge in larger districts. Keep in mind that the closer you can get to administering the survey to the entire target population, the more accurately your data will reflect the actual situation.

A description of your participants must be included in your final research report. For example, in the homework study mentioned above, the researcher could decide to collect data only from her high school chemistry class, since that is the class she teaches. Here is how she would define her sample. *The homework habits survey will be administered to all 40 students enrolled in high school chemistry at NU High School.*

Reflection 5.3

Now describe the samples that would be surveyed for the two research questions in Reflection 5.2.

Participants for Research Question 1 _____

_____

_____

Participants for Research Question 2 _____

_____

_____

Creating the Survey: Question Format

The first important step in creating your survey is to decide on the format for your survey questions. Think about what it is you want to accomplish. Make a decision if you can get the needed information by asking closed questions or if open-ended questions are needed. Open-ended questions generally allow the respondents to write their own answers, either by listing words or sentences. Closed questions have "yes–no," multiple choice, or rating scales in which you select your answer from the possibilities presented, rather than generating your own ideas. There are some advantages and disadvantages to each format (Table 5.1).

You should generally allow a "Don't Know" or "Not Applicable" response to all closed questions, except where you are certain that all respondents will have a clear answer. Sometimes labeling a response "Don't Know" may offer respondents the best

TABLE 5.1 Advantages and disadvantages of closed and open-ended questions

	Advantages	Disadvantages
Closed questions	• Can be answered quickly • Are easy to tally • Articulate respondents will not have an advantage over inarticulate respondents	• Can draw misleading conclusions because of the limited range of responses available • Do not allow respondents options in cases where they might say "It depends," or "Yes, but"
Open-ended questions	• Allows for more individual expression • No bias due to limited response range • Respondents can explain their answers	• Difficult and time-consuming to code • Responses may be misinterpreted

choice to answering your question. For the same reason, include "Other" or None" whenever a list of specific answers is presented. Leave a blank for respondents to write in their "Other" ideas. It is also possible to use a format that incorporates both open and closed questions in your survey.

Reflection 5.4

Select an appropriate format (open, closed or combination) for each of the research questions you posed earlier. Provide reasons for your selection that will make it clear why you selected the particular format for your survey instrument. For example:

Format for Research Question 1: *The homework habits survey will consist of mainly closed questions since I am most interested in time spent on homework, use of planners and, parent supervision of homework, all of which can be ascertained by giving students multiple choice ranges and choices to choose from.*

Now list the format you would use to collect data for each of the research questions you wrote above in Reflection 5.2. Provide a rationale for your choices.

Format for Research Question 1 _____

_____

_____

_____

Format for Research Question 2 _____

_____

_____

_____

Creating the Survey: Constructing Items

Once you have decided on a format, it is time to begin constructing survey items. For each item, ask yourself, "What could I learn from the answer to this question?" If you cannot give a satisfactory answer, leave the question out. Avoid the temptation to add a few more questions just because you are going to the trouble of making the survey anyway. If it is not relevant to your goals, don't ask!

A brief overview of several commonly-used categories of survey questions is given below. Be thinking about your research questions and which types of questions would best suit your needs as you read each selection.

Multiple Choice or Dichotomous

Use this type of question for situations in which specific responses can be predicted and placed with the choices, or when there is just a yes/no answer. For example, *Have you ever smoked?*, *Are you currently enrolled in an AP class?*, *Do you have a computer at home?* are all questions that can be answered with a yes/no response. Multiple choice items are a very popular type of survey questions because they are generally the easiest for a respondent to answer and the easiest to analyze. Write questions that accommodate all possible answers or the survey will be confusing and frustrating for respondents. For example, consider this question:

Where do you most frequently do your homework?

　a.　*In my bedroom.*
　b.　*At the kitchen table.*
　c.　*In our family room.*

Clearly there are many other places students could be working, for example, in their school study hall. Correct this potential problem by adding the necessary response categories. Problems in this area can usually be cleared up by interviewing several students while you are writing the survey to gather as many choices as possible. Always leave room for students to record an "other" response.

The following is an example of a question that can be answered in a multiple choice format:

Which was your favorite unit in science this year?

　a.　*Process Skills*
　b.　*Light & Sight*
　c.　*Ecology*
　d.　*Motion*

Open-Ended

Use this type of question for situations in which the respondents can answer in an unlimited number of ways. For example, *Why did you enroll in an AP class?*, *How do you react to bullies in school?*, *What do you consider to be the four best things about our school?*, *What do you consider to be the four biggest problems in our school?*

Reflection 5.5

Think of three sample questions that would be best asked using an open-ended question format.

Before you begin, it is important to note that research questions are very different from survey questions. The research questions are the questions guiding the study. The answers to these questions are not provided by the participants. Research questions are questions that researchers answer for themselves through the collection and analysis of data. In contrast, survey questions are the questions that researchers ask participants. Any question created for a participant to answer is not a research question.

Question 1 _____

_____

Question 2 _____

_____

Question 3 _____

_____

Creating the Survey: Scaled Responses

Scaled responses provide a limited number of predetermined responses to a survey item. The item is often in the form of a statement, such as:

Making friends is a very difficult thing to do at this school.
Having teachers in the hallways before, in-between, and after classes encourages good student behavior.
I have too much homework in most of my classes.

There are a variety of designs for scaled response. One of the most common scaled-response formats is the Likert scale. It is typically a five-point scale using the following format:

____ strongly agree ____ agree ____ neutral ____ disagree ____ strongly disagree

Reflection 5.6

Write three additional survey items as statements that could be used in conjunction with a scaled response format.

Statement 1 _____

_____

_____

(Continued)

(Continued)

Statement 2 _____

_____

_____

Statement 3 _____

_____

_____

Creating the Survey: Rating Scale

A rating scale is also frequently used on surveys, usually in situations in which you want respondents to rate something. For example, *Rate the amount of effort you place into each of the classes listed below, with "1" being no effort and "10" being a tremendous amount of effort.*

	Amount of effort									
US History	1	2	3	4	5	6	7	8	9	10
American Literature	1	2	3	4	5	6	7	8	9	10
Algebra	1	2	3	4	5	6	7	8	9	10
Chemistry	1	2	3	4	5	6	7	8	9	10

Don't change the rating method within the survey: use the same scale throughout. One final tip, be sure to ask only one question at a time. If you ask students the question "Are you satisfied with the quality and selection at our school cafeteria?", it is not clear which of the two factors, quality or selection, that respondents will refer to.

Reflection 5.7

Write at least two survey questions using a rating scale for each of the research questions you posed above in Reflection 5.2.

Survey Questions for Research Question 1

_____

_____

_____

Survey Questions for Research Question 2

_____

_____

_____

Creating the Survey: Title

Think of a title that will give the respondents some idea of the nature of the survey. Be careful not to create a title that would somehow indicate to the respondent your anticipated findings from the data.

Reflection 5.8

Indicate whether each of the following examples would be a good or poor title to use. Write a short justification for your choice.

"Kids with Good Homework Habits Get Better Grades" _____

_____

_____

"Homework Study" _____

_____

_____

"What's Your Homework Style" _____

_____

_____

"How Homework Habits Affect Grades" _____

_____

_____

Creating the Survey: Put Your Questions in Logical Order

The issues raised in one question can influence how people think about subsequent questions. It is usually best to ask general questions first, and progress to more specific questions. Writing a survey is similar to writing a good paper; transitions between questions should be smooth and questions that are similar should be grouped together. Surveys that jump from one unrelated question to another feel disjointed and are not likely to produce accurate results.

Creating the Survey: Write a Short Introduction

Give the respondents some idea of why you want their input. For example, are you interested in possibly changing some of your units or your mode of instruction? Are you trying to find out if there is a need for more communication with parents? Are you trying to improve student achievement or school climate? It is important that you convey to the respondents that you value their opinions. Reassure the respondents that their responses will remain confidential.

Creating the Survey: Write General Instructions

The exact instructions depend on the type of survey format you are using. It must be made clear to the respondents how to respond to each question, including an explanation for any rating scales that are being used.

Creating the Survey: Make Final Touches to Your Layout

Make sure your survey is attractive and easy to follow and complete. Read over your survey again. Ask a friend to complete the survey and pinpoint any potential problems.

4 Collect Data

Piloting Your Survey

Before administering the survey, pilot it by asking a few people from your sample population to complete the survey. For example, if parents are your target audience, ask several parents to complete the survey. Likewise, if students are your target audience, ask several students to complete the survey. Interview each test respondent after they have taken the survey. Find out if the directions were clear, if they understood the rating scale, or if there were any confusing points. If respondents skip certain questions, you should be able to find out why. Notice how long it takes to complete the survey. Based on the feedback you receive from your pilot sample respondents, make alterations in your survey.

Administer the Survey

Print copies of your survey and administer it to your sample. Make sure you have explained clearly how long they have to spend on it and how to return it to you: post, email?

5 Analyze

The findings from your survey should be more than a list of survey questions and their answers. The data should be tallied, organized, and analyzed into a format that summarizes the main findings quickly and easily. *Data is not capable of speaking for itself; it must be interpreted and explained by the researcher.* Researchers use a variety of tools to mine the data. For example, you may discover insights by using descriptive statistics like the mean, mode, and median; making comparisons among different groups of participants; and breaking down, combining, and recombining findings from different questions or different groups of participants. In short, researchers try to examine the data from as many perspectives as possible to gain insight. Most importantly, researchers look for the answer to their research question.

Observations

Below, you will find some sample data from a survey that asked high school students to report how much time they spent doing homework each night. The students could respond by saying they did more than two hours each night, 1–2 hours each night, 30–59 minutes each night, less than 30 minutes each night or that they never did homework. The data is listed below in frequency distributions. In each of the following frequency distributions, 9th indicates a ninth grader who reported doing more than two hours per night, 10th indicates a tenth grader who reported doing more than two hours homework each night, etc.

Reflection 5.9

Answer the questions associated with each frequency distribution.

Frequency of students who did more than two hours of homework each night:

> 9th, 9th, 9th, 9th, 9th, 9th, 10th, 10th, 10th, 10th, 10th, 11th, 11th, 12th, 12th

1 What is the mode (most frequently occurring grade level) for which doing more than two hours of homework is reported? *The mode refers to the most frequent occurrence of cases.*

_____

2 What is the median (the middle or average between two middle scores) grade level at which doing more than two hours of homework is reported? *The median refers to the midpoint number.* It can be calculated above by counting the total in the frequency distribution (15), then finding the midpoint, which would be the eighth number from either the top or bottom. In cases where there is an even number of scores, take the average of the two midpoint numbers. For example, if there were 16 total numbers, take the average of the eighth and ninth numbers.

_____

3 What is the mean grade level of students who do at least two hours of homework per night? Calculate the mean by adding all the grade levels (9+9+9+9 ...) and dividing by the total number (15).

_____

Frequency of students who did 1–2 hours of homework each night:

> 9th, 9th, 9th, 9th, 9th, 9th, 9th, 9th, 9th, 10th, 10th, 10th, 10th, 10th, 10th, 10th, 10th, 10th, 10th, 10th, 10th, 10th, 10th, 11th, 11th, 11th, 11th, 11th, 11th, 11th, 11th, 11th, 11th, 11th, 11th, 11th, 11th, 11th, 12th, 12th, 12th, 12th, 12th

4 What is the mode (most frequently occurring grade level) for which students are doing 1–2 hours of homework each night?

_____

5 What is the median (the middle or average between two middle scores) grade level at which doing more than two hours of homework is reported?

_____

(Continued)

(Continued)

6 What is the mean grade level of students who do at least two hours of homework per night?

_____

Frequency of students who did 30–59 minutes of homework each night:

9th, 9th, 9th, 9th, 10th, 10th, 10th, 10th, 10th, 10th, 10th, 11th, 11th, 11th, 11th, 11th, 11th, 11th, 11th, 12th, 12th, 12th, 12th, 12th

7 What is the mode (most frequently occurring grade level) for which students are doing 30–59 minutes of homework each night?

_____

8 What is the median (the middle or average between two middle scores) grade level at which students do 30–59 minutes of homework each night?

_____

9 What is the mean grade level of students who do 30–59 minutes of homework each night?

Frequency of students who did less than 30 minutes of homework each night:

9th, 10th, 10th, 11th, 11th, 11th, 11th, 12th, 12th, 12th, 12th, 12th, 12th, 12th, 12th, 12th

10 What is the mode (most frequently occurring grade level) for which students are doing less than 30 minutes of homework each night?

_____

11 What is the median (the middle or average between two middle scores) grade level at which students are doing less than 30 minutes of homework each night?

_____

12 What is the mean grade level of students who do less than 30 minutes of homework each night?

_____

Frequency of students who never did homework:

9th, 9th, 10th, 12th, 12th, 12th, 12th, 12th

13 What is the mode (most frequently occurring grade level) for which students are never doing homework?

_____

14 What is the median (the middle or average between two middle scores) grade level at which students are never doing homework?

_____

15 What is the mean grade level of students who never do homework each night?

_____

TABLE 5.2 A comparison of frequency of homework among high school students

Frequency of homework	Number of 9th graders	Number of 10th graders	Number of 11th graders	Number of 12th graders
More than 2 hrs each night	6 _____%	5 _____%	2 _____%	2 _____%
1–2 hrs each night	9 _____%	14 _____%	15 _____%	6 _____%
30–59 min each night	4 _____%	8 _____%	8 _____%	5 _____%
Less than 30 minutes each night	1 _____%	2 _____%	4 _____%	9 _____%
Never	2 _____%	1 _____%	0 _____%	6 _____%
Total	22	30	29	28

Reflection 5.10

Summarizing information in a table or with a graph can often provide insights that are not readily available when the data is simply listed in a frequency distribution. Study Table 5.2. Fill in the rest of Table 5.2 by calculating the percentages in the boxes.

Now let's combine the percentage data in a different way. Perhaps this new information can yield added insight.

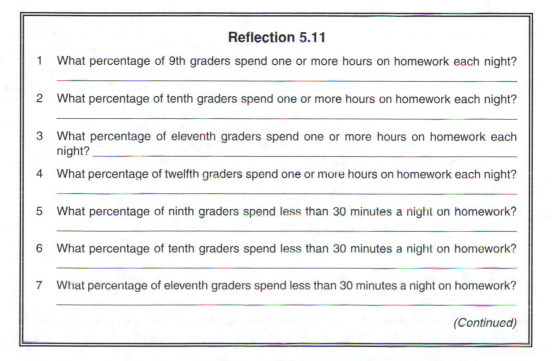

Reflection 5.11

1   What percentage of 9th graders spend one or more hours on homework each night?

_____

2   What percentage of tenth graders spend one or more hours on homework each night?

_____

3   What percentage of eleventh graders spend one or more hours on homework each night? _____

4   What percentage of twelfth graders spend one or more hours on homework each night?

_____

5   What percentage of ninth graders spend less than 30 minutes a night on homework?

_____

6   What percentage of tenth graders spend less than 30 minutes a night on homework?

_____

7   What percentage of eleventh graders spend less than 30 minutes a night on homework?

_____

(Continued)

(Continued)

8   What percentage of twelfth graders spend less than 30 minutes a night on homework?

_____

9   What percentage of total students spend more than two hours per night on homework?_____

10   What percentage of total students spend 1–2 hours per night on homework?_____

11   What percentage of total students spend 30–59 minutes per night on homework?_____

12   What percentage of total students spend less than 30 minutes per night on homework? _____

13   What percentage of total students never do homework?_____

6 Reflect

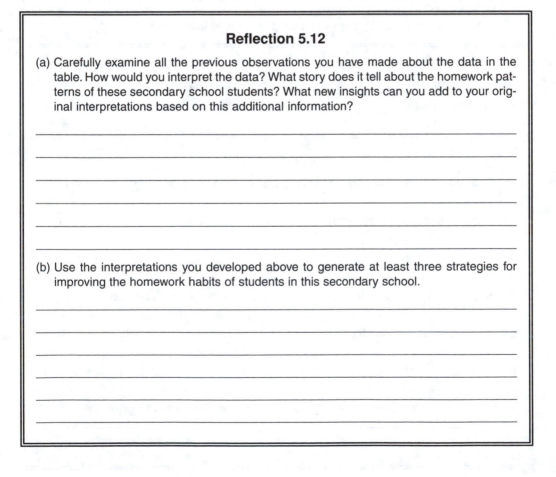

Reflection 5.12

(a) Carefully examine all the previous observations you have made about the data in the table. How would you interpret the data? What story does it tell about the homework patterns of these secondary school students? What new insights can you add to your original interpretations based on this additional information?

_____

_____

_____

_____

_____

_____

(b) Use the interpretations you developed above to generate at least three strategies for improving the homework habits of students in this secondary school.

_____

_____

_____

_____

_____

_____

(c) Justify your strategies based on the data you have analyzed, best practice, research-based strategies, or educational theory.

_____

_____

_____

_____

_____

_____

7 Summary

This chapter showed you how to conduct a survey. Like other forms of action research, you must create a research question and select research participants. When you construct your survey, you must decide on the type of format, questions, and responses. Using a scaled response enables the researcher to use descriptive statistics, such as the mean, median, mode, and percentages to summarize the data. Each different perspective adds to the number of observations that can be made from the data. Increased observations can lead to increased insight and a greater potential for developing new teahing strategies. You are now ready to design and conduct a survey action research project of your own design. As you work through your own project for the first time, it may also be helpful for you to revisit the information in this chapter to refresh your memory.

six
Using Interviews in Action Research

The teacher has opportunities for research, which, if seized, will not only powerfully and rapidly develop the technique of teaching, but will also react to vitalize and dignify the work of the individual teacher.

(Buckingham, 1926, p. iv)

1 Introduction

Interviews put the researcher in personal contact with the participant. Thus, they can provide an opportunity to ask follow-up questions, reveal rich insights into the thinking of the participants and help explain why your participants made the choices they did or how they think about a particular issue. Possible topics could include interviewing students about their thinking processes when solving problems, interviewing other teachers about the implementation of a new strategy, or interviewing parents about their literacy practices at home.

Interviews, like surveys, provide insights into the thinking of participants. However, interviews have an advantage over surveys because they involve fewer participants. Thus, there is an opportunity to ask follow-up questions that can more fully explore the why and the how of the interviewee's thinking.

It is important to remember that interviews are investigations into the thoughts and opinions of the participants, which may or may not be an accurate reflection of the actual situation. In addition, interviews are time-consuming and are therefore usually limited to just a few participants. Thus, a survey is much better for discovering the perceptions of a large number of participants, and the interview is much better for probing the perceptions of a small number of participants.

The aim of this chapter is to introduce you to the specific techniques needed to conduct your own interview action research study. As you read and respond to questions in the following sections, you will learn how to formulate a research question, select your participants, write interview questions, conduct the interview, record the data, and analyze the data after it has been collected. When you have finished this chapter, you will be ready to conduct your own interview action research project.

2 Steps in Conducting an Interview

The steps taken in conducting interviews are similar to other forms of research as shown below:

1   Plan
   (a) Establish the goals of the project. State your goals in the form of a research question. What is it that you want to learn?
   (b) Select your participants. Do you want to restrict your survey to students in your classroom, in your school, to a certain gender or ethnic background? Do you want to include students in other schools? What about parents and other teachers?
   (c) Determine which interview type best fits your research question. Create your interview protocol or interview guide.
   (d) Decide on a data recording format, whether it be note-taking, audio recording, or some combination.
   (e) Set a time and place for the interview.
2   Collect data
   (a) Conduct the interview.
3   Analyze
   (a) Analyze the interview data by making comparisons, viewing through differing conceptual lenses, and combining and recombining data.
4   Reflect
   (a) Interpret.
   (b) Develop new teaching strategies.
   (c) Justify your teaching strategies.
   (d) Write a summary report.

3 Types of Interviews

Structured interviews rely on the use of a list of questions developed by the researcher as a method of data collection. The theory behind this method is that each person is asked the same question in the same way so that any differences between answers are assumed to be real ones, and not the result of the interview situation itself. In this type of interview, the interviewer is considered to be totally neutral. No changes are made in the interview questions as the interview progresses; rather a script of questions with the same wording and question order is followed in each interview. There can be no prompting from the interviewer or requests for elaboration when an incomplete answer is received. The questions listed on the interview protocol are simply asked and the answers recorded.

The *semi-structured interview* leaves the interviewer more freedom to probe with follow-up questions. For example, when unexpected or interesting information comes out during the course of the interview, the interviewer can seek clarification and elaboration on the answers given. In some respects, this amounts to more of a dialog between the interviewer and interviewee.

In a *semi-structured interview,* the interviewer follows a fairly flexible process. The interviewer creates a list of questions of fairly specific topics to be covered, often referred to as an "interview guide." Questions may not follow in exactly the same order they were written on the interview guide. Questions that are not included in the guide may be asked, based on the responses of the respondents. But by and large, all of the questions will be asked with the wording written (or similar to that written) on the interview guide.

For example, in a semi-structured interview designed to investigate students' preferred learning styles, respondents may be asked to talk about their favorite and least favorite classes. Questions posed may ask students to recall memories about their best days in classes, their favorite projects and experiments, their most interesting assignments, their hardest exams, whether they felt they learned a lot, and the types of homework assignments they least enjoyed. As students answer these questions, the researcher may ask additional probing questions at any time he/she sees fit.

The *unstructured interview* is characterized by open-ended questions that are not necessarily prewritten. The researcher will typically prepare a list of specific points he/she would like information on. Questions can be posed from that list and can either be prepared ahead of time, or left to the moment. This method includes techniques such as life history, oral history, and biographical interviews. In an unstructured interview, the respondent has leeway to talk about the topic, and the researcher's role is to discover meaning by asking questions. The ability to ask questions that are based to some degree on the responses of the interviewee has the potential to provide a greater wealth of information and many times leads to a better understanding of the interviewee's point of view. There is a danger in this type of interview of the interviewer projecting his/her personal views into the interview. The researcher should allow the interviewee to do the majority of the talking.

The *group/focus interview* allows the researcher to explore group beliefs and dynamics around the issues and topics of interest. The participants are typically encouraged to talk to each other about the topic under consideration. The size of the group depends on the need to balance between too intimate and too impersonal.

It is possible to gain different results using group and individual interviews—especially when discussing issues involving collective interests, for example, school rules and harassment. Group interviews can provide a valuable insight into both social relations and the processes associated with group dynamics. At the same time, caution should be exercised in assuming the opinions are generalizable to the whole population.

4 Determining Your Research Question

As with other types of research introduced in this document, you must first establish your research question and identify the sample you would like to interview.

Once this is done, you can determine which interview type is most appropriate for your study.

Reflection 6.1

Using the format shown in the example below, write a research question, identify the type of interview you will use, and explain why you chose that type of interview.

Sample research question: *What types of bullying are occurring in our middle school?*

Interview type: A semi-structured interview format will be used, as it will likely be necessary to ask probing questions, based on student responses to the prepared set of question.

Before writing your answers, it is important to note that research questions are very different from interview questions.

Research question _____

_____

Interview type and rationale _____

_____

_____

_____

_____

Reflection 6.2

Create a research question for an interview of teachers concerning their beliefs on "constructivism." Identify the type of interview you would use and explain why you chose it.

Research question _____

_____

Interview type and rationale _____

_____

_____

_____

_____

---

5 Selecting Participants

Participants will necessarily be limited for an interview study so they should be selected with care. You may want to select participants based on their role as expert, e.g.

interviewing the principal of the school on policy decisions. You could also select participants in order to provide a contrast, e.g., interviewing high, middle, and low achievers about a newly implemented cooperative learning strategy. You may want to select participants who are typical of many other potential participants, e.g. three students out of 20 who scored well overall on the test but who all had difficulty with one particular section.

In the research report, you will create a "Participants" section. In this section, the individual participants are described in some detail. These details should all be relevant to the research question. For instance, if you are researching a student who is proficient in math, you should indicate age, gender, and the rationale for deciding this student was highly capable, e.g. test scores, classroom observations, homework assignments, etc.

Reflection 6.3

(a) Refer to the research questions and interview types you described in Reflections 6.1 and 6.2 to select a set of participants to interview in order to differentiate instruction in your classroom. What procedures would you use to select these participants?

_____

_____

_____

_____

(b) Describe a set of participants to interview in order to determine the community's awareness or reaction to a newly implemented reading program. Describe the procedures you would use to select these participants.

_____

_____

_____

_____

---

6 Writing Interview Questions

Once you have formulated your research question and have decided which type of interview would be best to use, you need to begin formulating the interview questions. Even for unstructured interviews, it is best to go into the interview with a prepared list of questions.

The order in which questions are presented can affect the respondents' willingness to provide detailed answers. Here are five tips for *sequencing the questions* in your interview.

1   Before asking about controversial matters (such as feelings and conclusions), first ask factual questions. With this approach, respondents can more easily engage in the interview before warming up to more personal matters. Factual questions address behaviors, knowledge and background. Questions about values, opinions, attitudes, beliefs and feelings require a deeper thought process on the respondents' part and that reflective thinking may

be difficult for some respondents to verbalize. Therefore, it is usually better to begin an interview with the factual-based questions and progress to the reflective questions as the interview progresses.

2   Don't begin by directly probing the issues you would like the interviewee to address. Start by asking more open-ended or unstructured questions that help the participant to talk about what they think is most important. This is an exciting part of the interview because it often elicits the most surprising and exciting information. If the interviewee does not address your issues in this part of the interview, you may still probe for them later. This approach enables you to find out what is most important to the interviewee, while still finding out about the issues that interest you.

3   Ask questions about the present before you ask questions about the past or future. It's usually easier for them to talk about the present and then work into the past or future from there.

4   The last questions might be to allow respondents to provide any other information they prefer to add and their impressions of the interview.

5   Before using them with the actual participants, it's a good idea to pilot your questions with similar type participants. This may clue you in to some of the surprises you will get in the interview.

The questions you create may be *structured*, *semi-structured*, or *unstructured*. An unstructured question is very open and allows the respondent to reply in a variety of ways, according to what they feel is most important. For example, "Could you describe your approach to teaching reading?" A structured question has a very specific focus and requires a very specific response. For example, "What are the benefits of using guided reading strategies?" A semi-structured question falls somewhere in between structured and unstructured questions.

When you create your questions, be aware that highly structured questions may be too leading, that is they may encourage the interviewee to give you the information she thinks you want to hear, thus resulting in inferior data. Conversely, questions that are too open-ended allow the interviewee to wander off topic, thus wasting the limited time available to conduct the interview. Try to create questions that neither lead the participants nor encourage off-topic responses.

Reflection 6.4

Below are three sets of questions. In each pair, one of the questions is less structured than the other. Identify the unstructured or less structured questions by putting a "U" in the blank and more structured questions by putting an "S" in the blank.

_____ 1   Do you use cooperative learning strategies in your classroom, and if so, to what degree have they been beneficial?

_____ 2   Could you explain the approach you take to facilitating peer interaction in your classroom?

_____ 3   What are your three most effective strategies for teaching literacy?

_____ 4   Describe your approach to literacy instruction.

_____ 5   What process did your group follow when making decisions?

_____ 6   How did your group decide who the reporter would be?

Your **interview questions** should emerge from your research question. Without a well-defined research question, your interview will lack focus. In formulating your interview questions, always try to visualize the possible responses you will receive, then build each subsequent interview question to allow the collection of more in depth information as the interview progresses. As you are composing your questions, keep in mind the pointers that were presented in the section on surveys. There are many similarities, but in the case of interview questions, you want the question to allow broad answers rather than "yes" and "no" answers.

Reflection 6.5

(a) Here is an example of an interview schedule for a semi-structured interview in which the research question was "What are the biggest frustrations experienced at school for middle school students?" The interview questions might include the following:

  1 What is it like being a seventh grader?

  2 Describe what would be a "perfect day" in your middle school class.

  3 What is your favorite thing about middle school?

  4 What is your least favorite thing about middle school?

  5 What pressures do you feel at school?

  6 What do you do for fun and entertainment?

Think about each of the questions posed above. Write three additional questions that would be logical additions to the interview schedule.

Interview Question 1 _____

_____

Interview Question 2 _____

_____

Interview Question 3 _____

_____

(b) Are there any of the example interview questions that you feel should be omitted? Which ones and why?

_____

_____

Reflection 6.6

Give yourself a little more practice at developing interview questions by writing at least four interview questions for each of the research questions posed below.

Research question: How do parents view the use of a computerized grading system for high school students?

Interview Question 1 _____

_____

Interview Question 2 _____

_____

Interview Question 3 _____

_____

Interview Question 4 _____

_____

Research question: What are student attitudes about the importance of standardized testing?

Interview Question 1 _____

_____

Interview Question 2 _____

_____

Interview Question 3 _____

_____

Interview Question 4 _____

_____

7 Preparation for the Interview

- *Choose a setting with little distraction and make time arrangements for conducting the interviews.* In selecting an interview location, it is best to avoid noisy rooms. If students are being interviewed, they may feel more comfortable in one of their own classrooms. Once you have selected a location, make arrangements for the room to be used and set up times during which the interviews will take place.
- *Prepare introductory remarks.* It is best to write either a script or an outline of what you will say. Highlights should include introducing yourself, explaining the purpose and format of the interview, and other remarks that will help to establish a person-to-person relationship. Explain (though only if it is true) that the information will be anonymous, and will be reported in ways that conceal the identity of individual respondent. Indicate clearly what use will be made of the information, and who will have access to it.
- *Decide how you will be recording the interview data.* Most interview data is recorded either with the use of a audio-recorder or through notes taken during the interview. Audio recording can assist interpretation as it allows the interviewer to concentrate on the conversation and record the non-verbal gestures. Audio recording also guards against interviewers substituting their own words for those of the person being interviewed. Conversely, some interviewees may find the tape recorder inhibiting and will not wish their conversations to be recorded. In certain situations, using an audio-recorder may simply not be possible. In these cases, the researcher has to take notes during the interview and write up those notes after the interview.

8 Conducting the Interview

- *Introductory remarks.* Use the notes from the "introductory remarks" you prepared prior to the interview. Remember to set the person being interviewed at ease. Do this by giving the person all of your attention. Remember to address terms of confidentiality and explain who will get access to their answers and how their answers will be analyzed. Make assurances that their names will remain confidential.

- *Explain the format of the interview.* Explain the type of interview you are conducting and its nature. When reviewing the format of the interview, be sure to let them know if you want them to ask questions during the interview or hold them until the end. Try to give the interviewee some idea about how long the interview will take.

- *Ask your interview questions.* Ask one question at a time. Attempt to remain as neutral as possible, that is, don't show strong emotional reactions to their responses. As the interview progresses, encourage responses with occasional nods of the head, "uh, huh"s, etc. Provide the transition between major topics, e.g., "we've been talking about (some topic) and now I'd like to move on to (another topic)." Be careful that you don't lose control of the interview. This can occur when respondents stray to another topic, take so long to answer a question that time begins to run out, or even begin asking questions to the interviewer.

- *Ask probing questions.* In unstructured or semi-structured interviews you may wish that respondents would elaborate on a specific subject. To encourage elaboration, try these strategies:
  - Take the last statement and turn it into a question.
  - Ask for examples.
  - Ask probing questions such as "Was this what you expected?", "How so/why not?", "How did you feel about this?", "Could you elaborate on this?", "You talked previously about ..., can you tell me more about that?"

- *Accurately record the data.* Use the plan you developed prior to the interview. Don't rely on your memory to recall the respondents' answers. If you are using a tape recorder, remember to ask for permission to record the interview and/or take notes. The greater eye contact and personal attention, the more likely you are to get accurate, in-depth responses, so don't be so focused on your note-taking that you no longer maintain eye contact with the speaker.

- *Immediately after the interview.* Read through your notes making sure everything is readable and makes sense. Make additional notes on your written notes that will clarify the data. Write down any observations made during the interview. For example, where did the interview occur and when? Was the respondent particularly nervous at any time? Were there any surprises during the interview? Did the tape recorder break?

9 Analyzing the Interview Data

In many respects, analyzing the interview data is more difficult than conducting the interviews. Your first task will be to get all the interview information on paper. If your data is recorded on a tape recorder, you must translate the recording into written text. You may either do this by typing an exact script of what was said or by developing categories into which you can directly place the responses as you listen to the tape. Once all the data is on paper, it must be sorted, categorized, and reduced to a few manageable themes through a coding process. *Coding* the data reduces the information from the interview into a manageable form and helps you to better understand and communicate your findings. It is not sufficient to simply report verbatim what the participants said.

The ways in which researchers begin to categorize data will depend upon the aims of their research and theoretical interests. To begin the coding process, researchers first read all of the transcripts. Next they develop a rough coding scheme based on themes that appear in multiple interviews. They look for themes (consistent ideas which emerged), incidence (when and where something occurred), patterns (the timing of occurrences), and trends (the frequency of patterns) (Macintyre, 2000). Grouping similar questions together may also be a way to organize interview responses into categories.

For practice sake, let's take a very simple and reduced example. (Hopefully, your participants will talk much more than the brief simulated responses shown in the example.) Below are five questions answered by three different participants: an administrator, an experienced teacher (15 years with a masters degree), and a first year teacher. Each participant has given a short response to each question. Read the interview questions and the participants' responses, then analyze the data by answering the questions that follow.

Interview Question 1: Tell me about how the No Child Left Behind legislation has affected you.

Principal: Initially, our greatest difficulty is getting the teachers to see the reason to change. Now we think everyone sees the benefits of making improvements based on student achievement. Our biggest problem now is determining the teaching strategies that will actually make a difference.

Experienced teacher: It has changed what I do with students and what I do when I'm with other teachers. I talk more about test strategies. I spend time talking with students about setting goals for their ITBS scores. Our grade level team now spends one or two meetings a month talking about student achievement data.

New teacher: I am just learning. Many of the items we talk about were not covered in my teacher education classes, like analyzing student achievement data on ITBS tests. So I am just trying to figure out where I fit in.

Interview Question 2: How has No Child Left Behind changed your practice?

Principal: We are now better able to link student achievement with specific teaching strategies. It has motivated our staff to look for new ways to motivate and engage students. We are more aware of how our students are performing and we are making decisions based on that information.

Experienced teacher: I find there is less time for enrichment activities, like art and music. In fact, even subject areas like Social Studies have received less attention as our emphasis has become increasingly focused on math and reading.

New teacher: This is my first year, so I can't say that I know it has changed anything. I am just trying to figure out how the district assesses students, what I am supposed to do, and how all these tests relate to my classroom teaching.

Interview Question 3: What impact has No Child left Behind had on how you view your students?

Principal: We are giving more attention to every single student. We have implemented several programs to improve student performance—like The Extended Day program. On the whole, I think many of our students now receive more individual attention than they would have previously.

Experienced teacher: I try to resist the idea that my students are nothing more than an standardized test score. Behind that number is a real person.

New teacher: It has made me more conscious of how widely the students vary in their skill levels. I can see how important it is to individualize instruction, although I'm not certain how I can find the time to do that with all of my other responsibilities.

Interview Question 4: What are the positives that have come out of this experience?

Principal: Looking at the data has helped us realize the changes we need to make in our building to improve student achievement. I think our future decisions will be much better informed if they are data driven.

Experienced teacher: I have benefited by collaborating with other teachers. I know more about assessment, and I am able to communicate better to parents about assessment. I think the Guided Reading program has helped a lot of students improve their reading skills. I also like being able to discuss different strategies we can implement based on what we see with student scores.

New teacher: I appreciate the opportunity to collaborate with more experienced teachers. It has helped me to learn about the school so much faster, and I have also picked up a number of valuable teaching strategies.

Interview Question 5: What are the negatives that have resulted from No Child Left Behind?

Principal: We are quite concerned about the punitive aspects of the No Child Left Behind. We're already underfunded so we cannot afford to lose any more resources. We're on the watch list so that has become an increasing source of anxiety.

Experienced teacher: Under the current legislation, the teacher is held more accountable without necessarily receiving more support from either the community or the Federal government. There is much more pressure on teachers to be accountable, but there is little additional support from the community. I also am worried that some of the strategies for improving our scores quickly may not be beneficial for students over the long run.

New teacher: There has just been so much for me to learn. Adding on all of this data analysis has just made it harder. I'm sure it will be helpful for me to know all of this in the future, but for now, I feel completely overwhelmed.

When analyzing data, it is important to consider the data from multiple perspectives. While many different approaches are possible, three are suggested here:

1   Examine the data to find comparisons and contrasts.
2   Combine and recombine the data in different patterns.
3   Frame and reframe the data through different conceptual or theoretical perspectives.

In Reflection 6.7, you are asked to examine the sample data above from each of these perspectives.

Reflection 6.7

(a) First, find comparisons and contrasts in the data above. For example, on which issues did the participants seem to all agree or share a similar experience? On which questions do the participants appear to differ in their perspectives because of their different roles or different experiential level in the school? Briefly summarize your findings.

_____

_____

_____

_____

_____

(b) Second, combine and recombine the interview responses in different ways. For example, pair the principal and the experienced teacher, the principal and the new teacher, and the experienced teacher and the new teacher to see on which issues they are similar and on which they are different. Briefly summarize your findings.

_____

_____

_____

_____

_____

(c) Third, examine the data from different conceptual perspectives to spark new insights. For instance, consider the interview comments from the themes of collaboration, accountability, and changes in practice. Briefly summarize your findings.

_____

_____

_____

_____

_____

Reflection 6.8

(a) Now that you have finished making your observations, review them carefully and interpret them. For example, you probably noted in your observations that both the experienced and new teacher commented favorably on teacher collaboration. This may be interpreted as meaning that both new and experienced teachers respond favorably to opportunities to collaborate with other teachers. Name at least two more interpretations that could be drawn from the data above.

_____

_____

_____

_____

_____

(b) At this point, you are ready to use your observations to develop new strategies for action. For instance, the comments of the new teacher suggest that the new teachers are overwhelmed when it comes to data analysis. Therefore, one practical implication from this set of interviews is that new teachers may need extra support when analyzing data. Name at least one more.

_____

_____

_____

_____

_____

_____

---

10 Summary

In this chapter, we have discussed the essential steps in designing and conducting an interview. Before conducting an interview, you must carefully compose a set of questions. It is usually better to use a semi-structured approach to asking questions. In a semi-structured approach, the interviewer begins with more unstructured or open-ended questions and gradually moves to more structured or leading questions. This approach accomplishes two purposes. First, the use of unstructured questions enables the interviewee to speak freely without being led by the researcher, thus enabling the discovery of information that the action researcher could not possibly have anticipated before the interview. Second, the use of structured questions enables the interviewer to target specific information with questions that directly address the research question. Semi-structured interviews also provide action researchers with an opportunity to ask follow-up or probing questions that permit a deeper exploration of the interviewee's responses.

The analysis of interview data is much different than the quantitative analysis associated with scaled responses on surveys. However, it is still important to try to distill and summarize the data in a way that identifies the most prevalent themes in the interviewee's comments. This can be accomplished by comparing and contrasting the data, by combining and recombining data, and by examining the data from different conceptual perspectives. You are now ready to design and conduct an interview action research project that addresses a problem in your classroom or school setting. As you work through your own project for the first time, it may also be helpful for you to revisit the information in this chapter to refresh your memory.

Part IV
Analyzing Test Results

Part IV consists of two chapters that each address the use of test results as action research data. Chapter 7 discusses the use of standardized achievement tests as a source of data for improving instruction. Four approaches to analyzing standardized achievement tests will be discussed: comparing to the norm, disaggregating data, trend analysis, and correlational analysis. Chapter 8 will discuss the use of pre and post tests for improving instructional strategies. Typically, pre and post tests are given more frequently than standardized achievement tests and are often more directly connected to the curriculum; therefore, they can complement standardized achievement test data by providing more timely and relevant information about instructional effectiveness.

seven

Standardized Test Analysis

Research, to be of use to teachers, requires that they test its theoretical implications in their classrooms. Much educational research, because of its allegiance to the psycho-statistical paradigm, expresses its findings as generalizations that cannot claim to offer guidance for action in particular settings. More supportive of teacher practice is research that either issues an hypothesis that can be tested in classrooms or that illuminates particular cases that can be judged against experience. Both can provide a stimulus to the planning of research-based inquiry in classrooms. Teachers who want to initiate research can appropriately employ an action research framework as a means of discovering hypotheses whose testing can lead to the improvement of practice and serve as an alternative route to the generation of theory.

(Jean Rudduck and David Hopkins, 1985, p. 7)

1 Introduction

Since the inception of the No Child Left Behind (NCLB) legislation, standardized achievement tests have become widely used as a primary source of data for making curricular and instructional decisions. They can serve as broad indicators of student performance in regards to thinking skills, reading comprehension, verbal ability, mathematical and science reasoning, and vocabulary. Examples of commercially prepared standardized tests would include the Iowa Test of Basic Skills (ITBS), the Stanford Achievement Test (SAT), the California Achievement Test (CAT), and the Comprehensive Test of Basic Skills (CTBS).

A half century ago, the use of standardized achievement test scores was limited to: (a) informing teachers and parents about students' achievement relative to their peers; (b) helping place students in appropriate programs; and (c) justifying the allocation of supplemental resources. However, public pressure to improve student achievement combined with advances in the technology of standardized test taking has led to many new uses of the standardized test results. Scores from standardized achievement tests can be used to make comparisons among students, across classes, within or among school buildings, school districts, or against the national norms. Standardized tests can provide useful information related to individual strengths and weaknesses in individual students, strengths and weaknesses in the curriculum, potential achievement gaps among various groups of students, and long-term trends regarding student achievement.

However, there is also the possibility that standardized achievement test scores can be misused. Concerned educators have warned that some uses are invalid and can have a negative impact on student learning, such as using them to evaluate schools, teachers, and as a requirement for grade promotion (Popham, 2001a, 2001b). There are also several limitations to using standardized achievement tests that need to be understood before drawing any definitive conclusions based upon this source of data. First, they do not provide information as specific as some other measures of student learning, such as classroom observations or assessment. Second, standardized achievement tests are usually given no more than once per year, thus the results cannot inform instruction on a daily, weekly, or even monthly basis. Third, the results are not always timely; it can take months before teachers have access to the results, and even more time before they are properly analyzed. Fourth, because of the long period between tests, it is difficult to establish the specific causes for improvement in student performance. Due to these limitations, standardized test results are used most effectively as broad indicators of student achievement and in conjunction with other types of action research data, especially classroom assessment data.

This chapter will describe four different approaches to analyzing standardized achievement tests for the purpose of improving instruction. They include comparing to the norm, disaggregating data, trend analysis, and correlational analysis. However, that does not mean that you should limit yourself to these four approaches. Action research methods continue to evolve, and the analyses described in this chapter are not intended to preclude other creative approaches to data analysis.

2 Steps in Analyzing Standardized Tests

As is the case with all forms of action research, action researchers need to formulate a plan for collecting and analyzing standardized achievement test data. The outline below serves as an overview of some suggested steps:

1 Plan
    (a) Make the purpose of the project explicit by stating the goals of your action research in the form of a research question. What is it that you want to learn?
    (b) Select your participants. Are you interested in the performance of students in your classroom, in your school, or in students belonging to a specific subgroup of the school population?
2 Collect data
    (a) Data collection and the procedures for distributing standardized achievement test scores are usually determined by school officials.

3   Analyze
  (a) Analyze the test scores using one of these four methods: comparing to the norm, dis-aggregating data, analyzing trends, or using a mixed analysis.
4   Reflect
  (a) Interpret the results of the analysis.
  (b) Use your interpretations to develop strategies for grouping, differentiated instruction, or a school-wide development plan.
  (c) Justify your teaching strategies.

In the following sections, you will be introduced to four analyses of standardized test data. The analysis will consist of making observations about the test scores, examining them from different perspectives, interpreting them, using them to develop new teaching strategies and using the sample data to justify the teaching strategies. Understanding these different approaches will increase your ability to utilize standardized achievement tests for action research purposes. It will also make it much easier to devise research questions and select participants for future projects.

3 Comparing to the Norm (by Individual)

Comparing to the norm is one of the most useful analyses for individual teachers. For ease of understanding, we have divided this approach into two sections: comparing individuals to the norm and comparing groups (e.g. classes, buildings, districts) to the norm. The purpose of comparing individuals to the norm is to analyze the strengths and weaknesses of individual students. A single year's worth of data can provide many valuable insights into student performance. The results can be utilized for providing remediation, designing differentiated instruction, grouping students, or filling gaps in the curriculum.

The *norm* refers to the performance of students in comparison to each other. Students are ranked normatively on standardized achievement tests by percentiles. Most standardized achievement tests take similar approaches to reporting their scores. However, the examples in this chapter will be based on two types of scores reported on the Iowa Test of Basic Skills (ITBS). They are percentile rank and grade equivalent. A student who scores in the 98th percentile has scored higher than 98% of the other students taking this exam. Similarly, a student who scores in the 10th percentile has scored higher than 10% of the students and lower than 90% of the students. By comparing one of your students' scores to the national norms, you are comparing your student to a group of students whose scores were used for the purpose of establishing norms. You can also compare students to the norms established for a single class, for your building, or for the entire district.

The *grade equivalent* is related to the percentile rank. For instance, a national percentile rank of 50 for third graders would be roughly equivalent to a grade equivalent of 3.8, for fourth graders it would be 4.8. (For further comparisons, see Hoover et al., 2003, p. 68.) Notice that both of these scores move upward as students mature. This allows educators to see progress and offers some advantages for creating trend lines on graphs. The grade equivalent also provides a readily accessible way for parents and teachers to judge student progress.

Reflection 7.1

(a) One approach to analyzing standardized test scores is to identify the strengths and weaknesses of individual students. The first step in this approach is to define what is meant by "strength" and "weakness." For example, examine the Iowa Test of Basic Skills scores of the individual student in Table 7.1.

TABLE 7.1 Example ITBS scores for an individual

Tests	GE	NPR
Vocabulary	10.2	95
Comprehension	8.4	75
Reading total	9.2	87
Spelling	10.3	90
Capitalization	7.2	60
Punctuation	14.9	99
Usage and expression	12.1	87
Language total	11.7	91
Concepts and estimation	5.5	39
Problem solving and interpretation	8.7	77
Mathematics total	7.0	63
CORE TOTAL	5.7	44
Social studies	6.9	59
Science	4.6	26
Maps and diagrams	8.8	75
Reference and materials	4.1	18
Sources of information total	6.2	50
COMPOSITE	5.7	44

Notes: GE = grade equivalent
NPR = National Percentile Rank

Proficiency in the state of Iowa is defined as scoring at or above the 40th percentile on the Iowa Test of Basic Skills. Therefore, students scoring below the 40th percentile would be seen as needing additional or alternative instruction to improve their score. If your school has established the 40th and 80th percentile as cutoffs for proficiency and mastery, then in which areas shown in Table 7.1 does the student need remedial instruction? In which areas would this student seem to benefit from enrichment activities?

_____

_____

_____

_____

_____

(b) Another approach is to divide the percentile ranks into quartiles. If your school considers scores between the 25th and 75th percentile as average, identify the strengths and weaknesses of this sixth grade student (above the 75th percentile and below the 25th percentile).

_____

_____

_____

(c) In what areas might you provide individual instruction for this student?

_____

_____

_____

(d) In what areas might you pair this student with a less able student?

_____

_____

_____

Plan: Writing a Research Question

Now that you have a little experience with comparing to the norm (individual) analysis, you should be able to design your own research question for this form of analysis. Research questions for this type of standardized achievement test analysis address the strengths and weaknesses of individual students. Two examples of appropriate research questions would be:

1   Which students are experiencing difficulties with computational math skills?
2   What are strong areas for individual students in my class?

Reflection 7.2

Think of two analyses that you could perform with your own data and write two more research questions for analyzing standardized achievement test scores using a comparing to the norm (by individual) analysis.

Research Question 1 _____

_____

Research Question 2 _____

_____

---

4 Comparing to the Norm (by Class, Grade Level, Building, or District)

Groups of students can also be compared to the norm. The purpose of this analysis would be to adjust lesson or unit plans at the classroom level or to adjust instructional programs at the grade, building, or district levels. The results can be used to identify gaps in the curriculum by identifying skill deficiencies.

Reflection 7.3

Examine the following hypothetical national percentile rank (NPR) scores from three different grade levels during the same year of testing in Table 7.2. Treat scores that are below the 40th percentile as not proficient, scores between the 40th and 80th percentile as proficient, and scores above the 80th percentile as attaining the mastery level.

TABLE 7.2 Example ITBS scores for three grade levels

Tests	4th grade	6th grade	8th grade
Vocabulary	38	46	42
Comprehension	36	44	45
Reading total	37	45	44
Word analysis	33	39	38
Spelling	44	46	49
Comprehension	40	48	52
Punctuation	42	47	51
Usage and expression	32	34	37
Language total	34	39	43
Concepts and estimation	28	26	31
Problem solving and interpretation	38	32	42
Computation	45	51	63
Mathematics total	36	39	41
CORE TOTAL	35	38	43
Social studies	42	51	58
Science	55	48	62
Maps and diagrams	68	63	81
Reference and materials	61	61	68
Sources of information	81	85	89
COMPOSITE	45	51	60

(a) What areas appear to require either more or improved instruction?

_____

_____

_____

_____

_____

(b) What areas appear to be satisfactorily addressed by current practice?

_____

_____

_____

_____

_____

Reflection 7.4

Now that you have identified your students' strengths and weaknesses, what types of strategies should you be searching for in the educational literature? Where would you look for new teaching strategies? How could you use the results of your analysis to develop a professional development plan for improving student learning?

_____

_____

_____

_____

_____

Plan: Writing a Research Question

Now that you have a little experience with comparing to the norm (by group) analysis, you should be able to design your own research question for this form of analysis. Research questions for this type of standardized achievement test analysis address the strengths and weaknesses of a collective group of students. Two examples of appropriate research questions would be:

1   What area of reading instruction could be targeted to impact the most significant growth in the ITBS reading scores?
2   When we examine the item analysis data for math on the ITBS, are the weaknesses discovered in problem solving consistent across all grades?

Reflection 7.5

Think of two analyses that you could perform with your own data and write two more research questions for analyzing standardized achievement test scores using a comparing to the norm (by group) analysis.

Research Question 1 _____

_____

Research Question 2 _____

_____

---

5 Disaggregating Data

The third form of analysis is _disaggregating data_. The purpose of disaggregating data is to determine the proportion of high and low performing students within either the total population or a particular group of students as indicated by standardized achievement test scores. The results of the analysis can be used: (a) to identify how well both low and high performing students are being served; (b) to compare the relative performance of different subgroups based on gender, ethnicity, or socioeconomic status; or (c) to discover the proportion of high and low performing students related to any skill or concept.

Analysis

Reflection 7.6

Examine the national percentile scores of sixth grade students from the following three groups of students, one Caucasian, one African-American, and one Asian.

Caucasian students

18, 98, 67, 55, 87, 65, 91, 95, 25, 34, 61, 72, 45, 55, 83, 89, 49, 56, 42, 76

African-American students

51, 15, 25, 67, 45, 45, 56, 82, 31, 45

Asian students

82, 56, 89, 65, 92, 80

Organize the scores from highest to lowest (frequency distribution) in the boxes below.

Caucasian students

African-American students

Asian students

Reflection 7.7

(a) Determine the percentage of scores above the 80th percentile, between the 40th and 79th percentile, and below the 40th percentile for the Caucasian students and write them in below.

_____

_____

_____

_____

(b) Determine the percentage of scores above the 80th percentile, between the 40th and 79th percentile, and below the 40th percentile for the African-American students and write them in below.

_____

_____

_____

_____

(c) Create a visual summary of your results and sketch it below. (Or you may want to construct a graph on the computer and attach the graph to your answers for this chapter. Specify its location in the space below.)

Reflection: Interpretations

Reflection 7.8

(a) By utilizing this approach, comparisons can be made between a variety of different groups, including gender differences, free and reduced lunch, and ethnicity. You should look carefully to compare the number of high performing to low performing students to see if these groups are all being served equitably. Based on your findings, what can you infer about the differences between these two groups?

_____

_____

_____

_____

(b) Use your interpretations to design new teaching strategies or sketch a plan for professional development based on this data. If you are not sure about what strategies are needed, where could you search for them and what search terms would you use?

_____

_____

_____

_____

(Continued)

(Continued)

(c) Use your knowledge of research-based instructional strategies and your experience to justify the strategies above.

_____

_____

_____

_____

Plan: Writing a Research Question

Now that you have a little experience with disaggregating data, you should be able to create your own research question for this form of analysis. Research questions for this type of standardized achievement test analysis address the strengths and weaknesses of a collective group of students. Two examples of appropriate research questions would be:

1   Is there a difference in the level of achievement between Caucasians, African-Americans, and Asian students in our school?
2   Are students on the free and reduced lunch program achieving at the same level as other students in the school?

Reflection 7.9

Think of two analyses that you could perform with your own data and write two more research questions for analyzing standardized achievement test scores by disaggregating data.

Research Question 1 _____

_____

Research Question 2 _____

_____

---

6 Analyzing Trends

A third approach to utilizing standardized test scores is to analyze trends. The purpose of analyzing trends is to determine whether instruction has positively influenced student achievement over time. The results of the analysis can be used to determine the effectiveness of program or school-wide interventions on composite, subject area, or skill area scores. A limitation of this approach is that it does not provide a very precise means for determining a cause and effect relationship between a single program intervention and

TABLE 7.3 Percentile rank to normal curve equivalent conversion table

Percentile Rank	NCE	Percentile Rank	NCE	Percentile Rank	NCE	Percentile Rank	NCE
1	1.0	26	36.5	51	50.5	76	64.9
2	6.7	27	37.1	52	51.1	77	65.6
3	10.4	28	37.1	53	51.6	78	66.3
4	13.1	29	38.3	54	52.1	79	67.0
5	15.4	30	39.0	55	52.6	80	67.7
6	17.3	31	39.6	56	53.2	81	68.5
7	18.9	32	40.1	57	53.7	82	69.3
8	20.4	33	40.7	58	54.2	83	70.1
9	21.8	34	41.3	59	54.8	84	70.9
10	23.0	35	41.9	60	55.3	85	71.8
11	24.2	36	42.5	61	55.9	86	72.8
12	25.3	37	43.0	62	56.4	87	73.7
13	26.3	38	43.6	63	57.0	88	74.7
14	27.2	39	44.1	64	57.5	89	75.8
15	28.2	40	44.7	65	58.1	90	77.0
16	29.1	41	45.2	66	58.7	91	78.2
17	29.9	42	45.8	67	59.3	92	79.6
18	30.0	43	46.3	68	59.9	93	81.1
19	31.5	44	46.8	69	60.4	94	82.7
20	32.3	45	47.4	70	61.0	95	84.6
21	33.0	46	47.9	71	61.7	96	86.9
22	33.7	47	48.4	72	62.3	97	89.6
23	34.4	48	48.9	73	62.9	98	93.3
24	35.1	49	49.5	74	63.5	99	99.0
25	35.8	50	50.0	75	64.2		

ITBS outcomes. Since schools employ a wide array of teaching strategies and instructional programs simultaneously, it is difficult to draw conclusions about the individual impact of each program based solely on information derived from a standardized achievement test.

Consider analyzing trend data over a three-year period for the following group of students. Your first step would be to summarize each year of individual scores with a single number. Although your first thought might be to calculate the average score for each year, there is a fundamental problem with that approach. *Percentile scores cannot be averaged accurately because they are measured on an ordinal scale (one without equal intervals between ranks).* The percentile intervals are closer together in the middle (where the raw scores tend to be bunched together) and farther apart at the end of the scale (where scores are spaced further apart). For example, three additional correct answers on a standardized achievement test may move a student from a percentile rank of 45 to a 55. In contrast, the same three correct answers may have little impact on the rank of a student at the 90th percentile.

Percentile scores, however, can be converted to Normal Curve Equivalents (NCE), which are based on an interval scale. This means that unlike percentile scores, NCE scores can be added, subtracted, multiplied, and divided. To convert a percentile score to an NCE, you would simply need to use a conversion table (see Table 7.3). After the percentile scores have been converted to NCE scores, they can be accurately added, divided, and averaged.

Analysis

However, a simpler approach and the one recommended in this manual is simply to use the median of the student scores. The median is the middle number of a string of scores. For instance, for the following list of scores 82, 78, 61, 43, 22, the median is 61 because 61 is the third or middle score. If there is an even number of scores in the list of scores, e.g., 82, 78, 63, 61, 43, 22, then average the two middle scores to find the median, which in this case would be 62.

Reflection 7.10

Take the composite reading scores listed below and determine the median. To determine the median score, first create a frequency distribution (organize from top to bottom scores).

Year 2006 26, 67, 33, 45, 91, 86, 22, 78, 68, 55, 68, 82, 10, 34, 48, 59, 90, 50, 72, 30

Year 2007 96, 82, 75, 33, 16, 38, 22, 87, 66, 81, 65, 34, 94, 22, 19, 28, 57, 61, 32, 73

Year 2008 65, 95, 85, 45, 84, 80, 47, 51, 55, 61, 56, 21, 73, 87, 67, 75, 43, 56, 58, 92

1   Frequency distribution for 2006 _____

2   Frequency distribution for 2007 _____

3   Frequency distribution for 2008 _____

4   Median for 2006 _____

5   Median for 2007 _____

6   Median for 2008 _____

(a) What do you notice about the trends you observed above?

(b) What conclusions could you draw about a guided reading program instituted during the 2006–2007 school year?

Plan: Writing a Research Question

Now that you have a little experience with trend analysis, you should be able to design your own research question for this form of analysis. Research questions for this type of standardized achievement test analysis address changes in performance over time. Two examples of appropriate research questions would be:

1   Have low SES seventh graders shown growth on the ITBS from the fall of 2004 to the fall of 2008 in the area of math concepts and estimation?

2   Have student scores in computational mathematics increased in the past three years?

Reflection 7.11

Think of two analyses that you could perform with your own data and write two more research questions for analyzing standardized achievement test scores using a trend analysis.

Research Question 1 _____

Research Question 2 _____

---

7 Mixed Analysis

You can also use a trend analysis in combination with a comparing to the norm or disaggregating data. You would simply use the same procedures for comparing to the norm or disaggregating data and then extend the analyses over a period of years. For example, comparing to the norm can be combined with a trend analysis by documenting improvement or decline in specific skill areas over time. Similarly, comparing the performance of student subgroups over a period of years would combine disaggregating data with a trend analysis.

Analysis – Multiple Perspectives

Analyzing trends in disaggregating data works a little differently.

Reflection 7.12

(a) Use the percentages of African-American students you found in Reflection 7.7 as data from 2006. For the year 2007, 20% were above the 80th percentile, 70% were between the 40th and 79th percentile, and 10% were below the 40th percentile. For the year 2008, 10% were above the 80th percentile, 80% were between the 40th and 79th percentile, and 10% were below the 40th percentile. Create a table showing this trend in the space below. (Or you may want to construct a graph on the computer and attach the graph to your answers for this chapter. Specify its location in the space below.)

(Continued)

(Continued)

(b) What can you conclude about the relative performance of African-American students over time?

_____

_____

_____

_____

_____

_____

Reflection 7.13

How could you use your interpretations to develop new teaching strategies? What types of strategies should you be searching for in the educational literature?

_____

_____

_____

_____

_____

_____

8 Correlating Data

The purpose of correlating data is to examine relationships between standardized achievement scores with other school measures, such as grades, attendance, discipline interventions, or other standardized achievement test scores. The results of this analysis could reveal: (a) high ability students who score well on standardized achievement tests but are not performing well in the classroom; (b) the relationship between students with low achievement scores and infrequent attendance; and (c) the relationship between standardized achievement scores and socio economic status, ethnicity, or gender. Findings from analyses such as these could provide insights regarding how to best serve different student populations within the school.

Reflection 7.14

In the example below, the percentile rank and GPA of a group of third graders is given. Each letter (e.g., A, B, C) represents an individual student. Each student's GPA and grade level equivalent has been given.

Percentile Rank

A (12), B(66), C(85), D (42), E(51), F (48), G(61), H(92), I(72)

C(3.4), G (2.2), H(3.1), E(3.0), D (2.5), I (3.3), A(1.7), F(2.9), B(3.1)

(a) Match the students' percentile rank with their GPA. Organize them from highest percentile rank to lowest.

(b) Do the students' percentile ranks appear to correlate with their GPA?

(c) What does that suggest to you?

(d) What observations can you make about individual students?

(e) What additional conclusions would you make if you knew that H and G were African-American students?

Plan: Writing a Research Question

Use the definition above to design your own research question for this form of analysis. Research questions for this type of standardized achievement test analysis address the strengths and weaknesses of a collective group of students. Two examples of appropriate research questions would be:

1   Have students who scored below the 40th percentile in second grade reading also earned similar scores in second grade math?
2   Is there a correlation between students' ITBS national percentile rank composite scores and their GPA?

Reflection 7.15

Think of two analyses that you could perform with your own data and write two more research questions for analyzing standardized achievement test scores using a trend analysis.

Research Question 1 _____

Research Question 2 _____

---

9 Summary

In this chapter, you learned four approaches to analyzing standardized achievement data. They are summarized as follows:

1   *Comparing to the norm* The purpose of comparing individuals to the norm is to analyze the strengths and weaknesses of individual students or groups of students. The purpose of comparing groups to the norm would be to adjust instruction for individuals or to adjust lesson or unit plans at the classroom, grade, building, or district levels. The results of this analysis can be used to identify gaps in the curriculum by identifying skill deficiencies.
2   *Disaggregating data* The purpose of disaggregating data is to determine the proportion of high and low performing students within either the total population or a particular group of students as indicated by standardized achievement test. The results of the analysis can be used: (a) to identify how well both low and high performing students are being served; (b) to compare the relative performance of different subgroups based on gender, ethnicity, or socioeconomic status; or (c) to discover the proportion of high and low performing students related to any skill or concept.
3   *Trend analysis* A trend analysis shows whether standardized achievement scores have improved over time for the purpose of determining whether an instructional intervention has positively influenced student achievement. The results of the analysis can be used to determine the effectiveness of program or school wide interventions on composite, subject area, or skill area scores.

4   *Correlational analysis* The purpose of a correlational analysis is to examine the relationship of standardized achievement scores to other school measures, such as grades, attendance, or discipline interventions. The results of a correlational analysis could identify students who score highly on standardized achievement tests but do not receive comparably high grades, a relationship between low achievement scores and infrequent attendance, or a relationship between standardized achievement scores and socio economic status, ethnicity, or gender. Findings could provide insights regarding how to best serve different student populations within the school.

The use of standardized achievement tests to measure student achievement has some limitations. Since, achievement tests are only administered once or twice per year, they offer limited insights regarding the development of new teaching strategies. They are more effectively utilized when combined with more frequent assessments of student work. When used together, standardized achievement data and classroom assessments provide a more complete picture of student achievement.

eight
Pre- and Post-Tests

There is growing support for the notion that research by teachers about their own classroom and school practices can serve as a powerful means of professional development
and can also contribute to the knowledge base in education.

(Marilyn Cochran-Smith and Susan L. Lytle, 1993, p. 85.)

1 Introduction

The aim of this chapter is to discuss the use of pre- and post-tests as action research data.
Examples would include pre- and post-tests constructed by teachers, curriculum-based tests
developed by a school district, or commercially prepared tests assembled by a textbook
publisher or testing agency. The type of analysis described in this chapter could also be
applied to any student performance that can be converted into a score through a rubric or
some other means. Examples would include rubric scores for skills or performances associated with speaking, writing, art, music, industrial arts, and physical activity.

Pre- and post-tests offer two benefits that compensate for the limitations of standardized achievement tests. They are given more frequently, and they are more closely
related to classroom instruction. Thus, many schools use pre- and post-tests as a way to
gauge improvement between the administration of standardized tests. Like standardized tests, pre- and post-tests also provide a useful approach for diagnosing strengths
and weaknesses of classes, individuals, or subgroups.

Also like standardized tests, pre- and post-tests are more useful for identifying problems with learning than suggesting new teaching strategies. Part of the reason for this
limitation is that converting student performances to numbers reduces the amount of

information available for analysis. Therefore, some of the nuances of student performance are not included in the analysis.

This chapter describes several approaches to analyzing pre- and post-tests. You will be shown how to determine gains in learning by comparing current achievement to pretests and baseline data; by comparing student subgroups with each other and the whole class, and by comparing individuals against the rest of the class. The information and exercises in this chapter will be focused on analyzing pre- and post-tests for the purpose of generating new teaching strategies. It will not be directed towards constructing tests or rubrics. For more information on constructing tests and rubrics, you should consult a text on educational assessment.

2 Steps in Comparing Pre- and Post-Tests

To effectively analyze pre- and post-tests, you will need a plan for your research. Below is an overview of some suggested steps:

1   Plan
  (a) Make the purpose of the project explicit by stating the goals of your action research in the form of a research question. What is it that you want to learn?
  (b) Select your participants. Do you want to restrict your analysis to students in your classroom, to your school, to a certain gender or ethnic background? Do you want to make comparisons across grade levels?
2   Collect Data
  (a) Administer the pre-test.
  (b) Teach.
  (c) Administer the post-test.
3   Analyze
  (a) Analyze the test scores by comparing pre and post-tests for the whole class, by comparing post assessment data for the whole class to baseline data, by comparing subgroup data to whole class data, and by comparing individual test results to whole class data.
4   Reflect
  (a) Interpret your observations.
  (b) Use the results of your analysis to devise new teaching strategies or a new action plan.
  (c) Justify your teaching strategies.
  (d) Write a summary report.

3 Comparing Pre- and Post-Tests

Post-tests data can provide helpful insights into student learning and the effectiveness of teaching strategies. A *post-test* is a test given after a teaching intervention. For example, imagine a situation in which you taught a unit on the constitution. At the end of the unit, you wanted to know how successful your teaching had been, so you gave a multiple choice post-test.

Reflection 8.1

Your students received an average score of 84%. What could you conclude about student learning based on that score?

_____

_____

_____

A *pre-test* is given before the unit or lesson begins. Pre-test results can identify strengths and weaknesses of students, thereby giving teachers a chance to adjust their instruction before beginning the unit. A limitation to pre-tests is the extra effort in creating and grading them. This extra burden can be somewhat lightened by using an old chapter test, previously created tests, or using the same pre-test as the post-test. The pre-test can also be compared with the post-test to provide further insight.

Reflection 8.2

For instance, what if you knew that in addition to a post-test score of 84%, your students had scored an average of 75% on a pre-test. What would you now say about the gain in student learning?

_____

_____

_____

Reflection 8.3

What if the pre-test score averaged 35%? In what way would that inform your previous conclusions?

_____

_____

_____

Baseline data could be used as another point of reference for post-test scores. Baseline data are the pre- and post-test scores from previous teaching interventions. For example, they could be the test scores from similar tests given earlier in the year, such as using the average scores from several spelling tests. Or they could be the average scores from a single unit, such as the test results from the previous years' unit on long division. Like pretest scores, baseline data can be compared with post-test results. A better comparison can be made when the two sources of data share a similar format. For example, if the baseline data consist of observations of children sorting pictures, then the post-test data should as well.

Reflection 8.4

(a) After receiving pre-test scores that averaged 35% correct and post-test scores that averaged 85% correct, you re-teach the unit the following year. Your scores are 25% correct on the pre-test and 85% correct on the post-test. What can you now say about the gains in student learning?

_____

_____

_____

(b) What if your second year classes scored 35% on the pre-test and 95% on the post-test? How could your baseline data (scores from the first year) aid you in drawing conclusions about the second year class?

_____

_____

_____

(c) What if the pre-test scores from the three previous years averaged 25, 35, and 45%? The post-test scores average 75, 85, and 95%. How could you use this information to draw conclusions about the gains in student learning?

_____

_____

_____

---

4 Comparing Subgroups

Learning goals and strategies can be evaluated in relation to their impact on subgroups of the larger group. Subgroup data could be disaggregated based on ability, gender, ethnicity, or other identifiers.

Reflection 8.5

Say that Subgroup B scored 25% on the pre-test and subgroup A scored 45%. At the end of the unit, Subgroup B averaged 70% and Subgroup A averaged 95% correct on the post-test. The entire class averaged 35% correct on the pre-test and 90% correct on the post-test. Create a graph in the space below that compares the increase in learning from pre- to post-test of the whole class to each subgroup. (Or you may want to construct a graph on

(Continued)

(Continued)

the computer and attach the graph to your answers for this chapter. Specify its location in the space below.)

Reflection 8.6

(a) Based on the graphs and the numerical data above, how well did the subgroups perform in relation to each other and the whole class?

_____

_____

_____

(b) How do the two subgroups differ in their need for instructional strategies?

_____

_____

_____

5 Individual Adaptations

Learning goals and strategies can be evaluated in relation to individuals as well as the whole class.

Reflection 8.7

(a) Say that two of your students scored 10% correct on the pre-test. Based on these results, you provide individual adaptations for these students. At the end of the unit, one of the students scored a 85% correct, the other scored a 40% correct. The rest of the class averaged 35% correct on the pre-test and 85% correct on the post-test. In the space below, create a graph that compares the increase in learning from pre to post-test of the whole class to each individual student. (Or you may want to construct a graph on the computer and attach the graph to your answers for this chapter. Specify its location in the space below.)

(b) Based on the graphs and the numerical data above, how well did the individual adaptations work for each of these two students?

_____

_____

_____

6 Evaluating Teaching Strategies

There are several approaches to using pre- and post-tests to evaluate teaching strategies. One approach would be to introduce a single new strategy, such as cooperative learning. Significant gains in learning compared to the previous baseline would indicate that the cooperative learning strategy had made the difference. The fewer changes you made in the other teaching strategies, the more confident you can be that the change in strategies caused a change in student performance. The more strategies utilized, the less certain it is that one particular strategy changed anything.

Reflection 8.8

If you only changed one strategy—added cooperative learning—in a unit on which students averaged 87% correct compared to previous years' baseline average of 75%, what would you conclude about the effectiveness of cooperative learning as a teaching strategy for this unit?

_____

_____

_____

Pre- and post-tests can also be utilized to evaluate teaching strategies by giving them immediately before and after the teaching strategy is utilized, for example, a quiz immediately before trying cooperative groups and a quiz after implementing cooperative groups. No other teaching intervention should be implemented between the pre- and post-test. A similar approach would be to evaluate test items in relation to your learning goals.

Write your test items so they apply to specific learning goals, then use this information to evaluate the strategies you used to accomplish each learning goal.

Reflection 8.9

On the pre-test you ask 10 questions on the causes of the Civil War. The students average two correct. During the unit on the Civil War a variety of teaching strategies were used, but all information on the causes of the Civil War was covered through cooperative group

(Continued)

(Continued)

research projects and presentations. On the post-test 10 questions were asked on the causes of the Civil War, and students scored an average of 8 correct. What would you conclude about the effectiveness of using cooperative learning during this teaching unit?

_____

_____

_____

7 Developing New Teaching Strategies

Pre- and post-test analyses are most useful for evaluating existing teaching strategies. If you would like to use test data to develop new strategies, it is necessary to take a closer look at your test items. One approach would be to conduct an item analysis of the test. An *item analysis* is a close examination of your test questions, usually your questions with the most incorrect responses. The wording and specific requirements of the question may provide insight into the cause of the student's incorrect response. For example, the following question was asked on a seventh grade language arts test.

> *The following pairs of words can best be described as:*
> *a. antonyms b. synonyms c. homonyms d. palindromes*
>
> *ate: eight   aisle: isle   ant: aunt*

The teacher observed that 50% of the class missed this question. Of those who missed the question, 60% answered antonym, 30% answered palindrome, and 10% answered synonym.

Reflection 8.10

(a) Based on the teacher's observations, what inferences can you draw concerning the students' understanding of antonyms, synonyms, homonyms, and palindromes?

_____

_____

_____

(b) Based on your interpretation of student understanding, what new teaching strategies would you recommend?

_____

_____

_____

(c) Justify the teaching strategies you have recommended using the data, recommendations for best practice, educational research, and/or educational theory.

_____

_____

_____

---

8 Deciding on a Research Question

Now that you have had a chance to examine different approaches to using pre- and post-assessment data, consider how you use these sources of data to design an action research study. Like an analysis of a standardized achievement test, you may create comparisons among individuals, subgroups, classes, or to the baseline from previous years. The research questions associated with this form of data analysis will probably link student performance and an instructional strategy in relation to one or more learning goals in some way. Your research question should be direct and narrowly focused. Don't take on a topic that is so broad you will not have time to complete the analysis or reach a conclusion. Two examples of appropriate research questions would be:

1   Did the introduction of cooperative learning improve student understanding of the causes of the Civil War?
2   Are there particular subgroups of students in the class that benefit more from the use of cooperative learning than other student subgroups?

Reflection 8.11

Now write two more research questions for action research studies you would be interested in conducting and that would involve the use of pre-and post-test analysis.

Research Question 1 _____

Research Question 2 _____

---

9 Summary

This chapter showed you how to evaluate instructional strategies by comparing pre-tests, post-tests, and baseline data on the whole class, subgroup, and individual level. This provides a way to see how whole classes have done in relation to previous classes, how subgroups compare to each other, and how individuals are doing compared to the class average. Pre- and post-test data can also complement standardized achievement data by providing more timely information on student progress. Like standardized tests, they also provide an effective means of evaluating current strategies. Teaching strategies can be evaluated by trying one new strategy, by pre- and post-testing immediately before and after using the strategy, and by using a comparison group. To use pre- and post-testing to develop new strategies, look more specifically at test items in relation to the learning goals, at the specific construction of items, and at the pattern of student answers.

Part V
Talking and Writing about Action Research

Part V consists of two chapters that address communication in action research. Chapter 9 describes how to collaborate in a teacher study group when analyzing action research data. In this chapter, you will learn how to create a dialogue around action research through your participation in a teacher study group. For that conversation to be fully effective, it needs to follow a systematic, step-by-step process in which your thinking becomes explicit, public, and subject to review. Chapter 10 will show you how to communicate your findings by writing them up in an action research report. Creating a written report provides a record of your work and an important source of information for others. Even more importantly, the process of writing can help clarify and extend your insight into the data.

nine
Collaborating on
Action Research

Teachers learn best by studying, doing, and reflecting; by collaborating with other teachers; by looking closely at students and their work; and by sharing what they see.

(Linda Darling-Hammond, 1999, p. 8)

1 Introduction

All types of research are communal in nature, and action research has been associated with collaboration since its inception. When working collaboratively, teachers are often organized into teacher study groups consisting of four or five teachers, one of whom may be designated as the facilitator. Teacher study groups could include building teams, grade level teams, or any formal or informal gathering of teachers whose purpose is to discuss teaching and learning. A variety of topics can be undertaken by teacher study groups, including those related to school change, issues of equity, and problems associated with site based management. In this book, the primary focus is on instructional improvement.

Collaboration offers several advantages for conducting action research. First, it can reinforce the systematic thinking associated with action research, such as the process of plan, act, observe, and reflect that has been reiterated throughout the previous chapters of this book. Second, it provides a venue for making your research public and explicit. Communicating your research findings to others and engaging with them in a thoughtful dialogue inevitably sharpens your thinking and improves the quality of the research. Third, collaboration establishes a culture for continuous school improvement and a means for rapidly disseminating new teaching strategies.

There are several limitations or barriers to collaboration among teachers. Two of the most prominent are a lack of time and a lack of focus. Another key consideration is the establishment of a positive climate of acceptance and trust among group members. This is crucial for establishing the level of trust needed to share potentially sensitive information from our classrooms. Addressing these limitations will be discussed in the chapter.

The primary purpose of this chapter is to show teachers how to establish, structure, and manage a teacher study group. Specific topics include creating a systematic approach to managing time, establishing group norms, analyzing data, and facilitating interactions among group members. By the end of this chapter, you should know how to move through a collegial discussion of action research data in a focused, systematic, and unthreatening way.

2 Establishing Group Norms

Little, Gearhart, Curry, and Kafka (2003) have suggested that concerns for personal comfort and collegial relationships can be a significant barrier to collaboration. Therefore, a primary task when organizing a teacher study group is to establish the norms for conducting a collaborative conversation. Group norms are the procedures that govern the interactions among group members, such as how study team members manage their time, how they talk to one another, and how they structure the meetings. They are the single most important factor in determining the group's harmony, efficiency, and productivity. Examples of group norms would be ensuring that everyone has a chance to speak, that professional courtesy will be maintained at all times, and that group members will be nonjudgmental in regards to their colleagues' teaching.

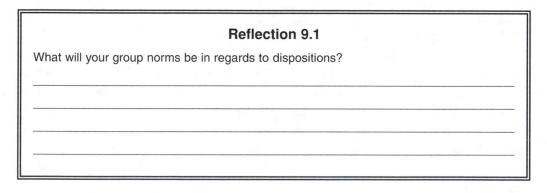

Reflection 9.1

What will your group norms be in regards to dispositions?

The group may operate more effectively if one person is designated as a facilitator in order to set the agenda and keep the group on task. Effective facilitators should be knowledgeable and skilled enough to model communication skills and data analysis procedures for other members of the group. Yet the facilitator must also be able to assume a nondirective, more democratic style of leadership to encourage the participation of other group members. In addition, the facilitator must strive to maintain a positive, comfortable atmosphere while simultaneously challenging other members of the group to think more deeply. Study groups might want to consider rotating the role of facilitator among group members because serving as a facilitator offers several benefits.

To stimulate the interactions among study team members, three specific conversational moves have been suggested by Langer, Colton, and Goff (2003): pausing, paraphrasing, and probing.

1   *Pausing* is simply waiting and thinking before speaking. The facilitator or any other group member is trying to understand first, trying to be understood second. It is important to listen carefully to others, to remain nonjudgmental so that you do not rule out new ideas without due consideration, and to inquire for the purpose of learning.

2   *Paraphrasing* is rephrasing what you have heard in order to make sure you understood correctly. Using this technique could save you from wasting time spent in misunderstanding. It could also help you clarify your assumptions or the unspoken premises that lie underneath what you are saying.

3   *Probing* is asking a series of questions to clarify what another person is saying. This technique can help another person better articulate what they are trying to say. Sometimes what they are saying can be clarified with examples. This can enhance shared understanding.

3 Managing Time

Time is always a scarce resource for teachers and can serve as a significant barrier to the successful implementation of a teacher study group (Cochran-Smith & Lytle, 1999; Little et al., 2003). Little et al. (2003) have suggested that a significant barrier to effective teacher study groups is scarce time. To begin a teacher study group, enough time must be allotted to meet for at least an hour once or twice a month. If the interval between meetings is longer than a month, the study group will probably lose momentum. Too much time will be spent trying to recall what happened at previous meetings at the expense of moving forward in a productive fashion. It is best that the meetings occur during the school day or as part of regular school activities, so that other concerns, like extracurricular responsibilities or family obligations, don't cause absences or the cancellation of meetings.

Reflection 9.2

Sketch out a plan for the year based on 9 months, one or two hourly meetings per month. How will you organize your time?

_____

_____

_____

---

4 Choosing Your Data

The first decision to make is what data you will use. At this point in the book, you should understand that different forms of data reveal different insights. No one research methodology is superior or inferior to other forms of action research. Each research method provides a different piece of the puzzle so that none are superior or inferior measures of "truth." In addition, it is important to know that combining different methods and approaches in your action research study will give you more perspectives on the effectiveness of your teaching strategies. As you continue to use these various methods, you will grow in your understanding of the advantages and limitations of each method. The following is a summary of the action research methods discussed earlier in the book.

- Observing Students and their Work
- Observing Teachers
- Conducting Surveys
- Conducting Interviews
- Analyzing Standardized Achievement Tests
- Analyzing Pre- and Post-Tests.

For a review of the above, see Chapter 2, pp. 29–30.

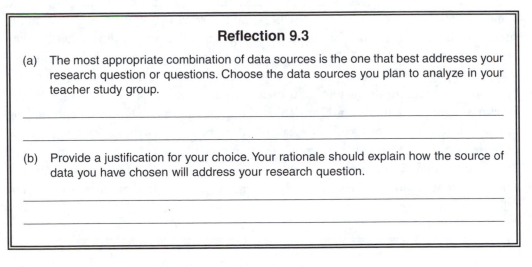

Reflection 9.3

(a) The most appropriate combination of data sources is the one that best addresses your research question or questions. Choose the data sources you plan to analyze in your teacher study group.

_____

_____

(b) Provide a justification for your choice. Your rationale should explain how the source of data you have chosen will address your research question.

_____

_____

5 Structuring the Discussion

Structuring the conversation is also critical to performing a successful analysis. To increase the efficiency of study team discussions, it is important to follow a systematic process. Being systematic means that teachers follow a series of steps in their analysis, that they are aware of the thinking that needs to be done in each of these steps, and each step of the analysis is fully explored. There are two primary advantages to following a step-by-step process. First, it is time efficient. Within the hour or so that study team members have to examine their classroom interactions, they must establish and follow a focused agenda or the time will quickly be squandered without accomplishing very much of value. Using time wisely also means that individual meetings must be carefully planned and executed. Following a well-defined set agenda for analyzing data provides a means for organizing individual meetings, for keeping the meetings focused, and for managing the process.

Second, a structured conversation leads to better results. Since there are different goals accomplished at each step of the analysis, carefully examining all the possibilities in the data before moving on to the next step assures a more thorough treatment of the data. In addition, study team members must be able to justify the decisions they make at each step of the process. By making their thinking public, teacher researchers set the conditions for creating better awareness of their decision making in the classroom, which can lead to opportunities to improve both their thinking and their practice. The four-step approach to data analysis recommended throughout the book will also serve as the structural basis for collaborative conversations: (1) plan; (2) collect data; (3) analyze; and (4) reflect.

The following sections will describe how a collaborative conversation can be structured around the four-step cycle of the action research. As you read through the descriptions, you will be asked to create your own plan for structuring the teacher study group conversation. As part of the plan you will be asked to describe the facilitator's role in each section of the discussion, to supply sample questions that group members could ask each other during that phase of the discussion, and to list any materials you would create to support the discussion. The plan you create should be appropriate for your research question, your sources of data, and the time you have available.

The Action Research Plan

The first step of the analysis is to establish the initial plan for the study, including information about the teacher's purpose, the participants, the setting, and the sources of data:

1   The teacher's purpose could either be related to teaching (the objective for the lesson) or the research (the particular problem she is investigating).
2   The participants in a study of classroom interactions will usually be the students. The kind of information that is relevant to an inquiry related to classroom discourse could include their grade level, their gender, their ethnicity, or their ability levels. Other possible participants could also include teachers, administrators, and parents.
3   The setting will generally refer to the classroom, school, or possibly community environment. It could include physical descriptions, a description of the psychological environment, or descriptions of other environmental factors.
4   The sources of data could include standardized achievement tests, pre- and post-tests, observations of students and teachers, surveys, or interviews.

The information above serves as the foundation to the discussion and should be made clear before trying to engage in the analysis for three reasons. First, it is important part of communicating within the teacher study group. Without an understanding of the teacher's purposes, the grade level of students, or the school environment, other study group members will not be able to ask effective and stimulating questions or reach significant insights. Second, teaching and learning always occur in specific locations under specific conditions. Knowing the gender, age, or ability level of students can often have a profound effect on the conclusions that are drawn from a set of data. It is also helpful to understand the purposes of the teacher, what she was trying to accomplish, and what she anticipated would happen during the lesson. Finally, it can also be helpful to know what kind of data was collected and how it was collected. As discussed earlier in previous chapters, different insights can be gained from analyzing videotapes than from analyzing lesson plans. As in every step of the process, the thoroughness with which study team members attend to the details here will have an impact on the conclusions that you draw from the next phases of the discussion.

To facilitate the study team's understanding of the action research plan, the facilitator or other study team members could pose questions to the teacher who is presenting the data. The purpose of these questions is to probe for additional details concerning the context of the study. Questions that could be asked during the discussion to help clarify the plan could include:

1   What were your goals for the project?
2   Who were the participants?
3   What was the context of the lesson?
4   What did you hope would happen during the lesson?

Reflection 9.4

Provide two more example questions that could be asked during the Plan part of the discussion.

_____

_____

_____

Data Collection

The group should review how the data was collected during the study so that everyone is fully acquainted with the context of the action research. First, there should be a complete description of the teaching procedures. Second, the procedures for collecting data should be fully described. Knowing how the data was collected will help the teacher study group make better decisions about the usefulness and significance of the data. Questions that could be asked during the discussion to help clarify how the data was collected could include:

1   What instructional strategies did you use to reach these goals?
2   How was data collected during your action research study?

Reflection 9.5

Provide two more example questions that could be asked during the Data Collection part of the discussion.

_____

_____

_____

Analysis

In the Analysis phase of the discussion the study group examines the data together. As discussed previously, the data could include teacher lesson plans, samples of student writing, observations of classroom interactions, or audio and videotapes of classroom interactions. The primary purpose of this step of the analysis is to make and record as many relevant factual observations about the data as possible. The goal of teacher researchers is to find new phenomena that have been overlooked previously, perhaps because they have been considered unimportant or perhaps because our eyes were not trained to see it. Typically, we human beings tend to see focus on what we value as important or what we are conditioned to see. So it requires a conscious decision to withhold judgment and the self-discipline to consider other possibilities before drawing a conclusion. Withholding judgment and remaining impartial are critical to the discovery of new information. Once you have made a judgment or a decision, thinking stops.

Instead, teacher researchers must make a concerted effort to look at the data in new ways and to examine more closely what had previously seemed trivial. Otherwise, we are likely to simply see what we have always seen or to disregard potentially valuable information. So when making observations about the data, try systematically combing through the data to find what has been previously ignored. The significance of the observations can be decided in the next phase of the discussion. Making more observations at this step of the process increases the possibility of gaining more insight during the reflection phase. To interpret the data in new ways, it must be seen in new ways. Questions that could be asked during the discussion to help clarify how the data was analyzed could include:

1   What are you seeing in this sample of student writing?
2   How would you summarize these tallies of classroom interaction?
3   What do you observe in these interactions?

Reflection 9.6

Provide two more example questions that could be asked during the Analysis part of the discussion.

_____

_____

_____

Reflections: Interpretations

In this part of the analysis, the study group members examine their observations for patterns and relationships. The discovery of those relationships gives meaning to your data. Just as you tried to multiply your observations in the previous phase of the discussion, in this phase of the discussion, try to multiply your interpretations. Consider as many different ways to connect and explain the data as you possibly can. The objective of data analysis is not to find a single truth; the purpose is to better understand the complex interrelationships governing teacher and student interactions and to use that understanding to improve teaching strategies in the next phase of the discussion. Questions that could be asked during the discussion to help generate multiple interpretations could include:

1   What might explain why the student is performing this way?
2   What do these interactions tell you about the effect of the instructional strategies you used?

Reflections: Develop New Teaching Strategies

One of the primary purposes of analyzing classroom interactions in study teams is to develop decision-making skills in the classroom. The purpose of this step of the analysis is to consider the patterns of interaction identified in the previous section and then develop new ways of responding and interacting within those patterns. In this phase of the discussion, the study team will set new goals for classroom interactions, then create a plan and a set of strategies for meeting those goals. Your goal should be to generate as many alternative strategies as possible, then to select the most promising one or ones for implementation. The advantage of developing multiple strategies is twofold. First, keeping your mind open to a variety of possibilities may prevent a premature negative judgment regarding a potentially effective strategy. Initially, it is important to generate possibilities; later, you can select among the most promising approaches. Second, no single approach to teaching will ever be effective because of the widely varying contexts and interactions that are a part of teaching. It is always helpful to have additional strategies in reserve for special students or situations.

As part of your teacher study group, you may want to design a plan for developing new strategies. There are four sources to developing new strategies, and they include:

1   Through direct observations of students and their work, e.g., examining student writing, student speaking, or observing student behavior.
2   By sharing strategies among teachers.
3   Through searching and reading through the educational literature.
4   Through professional inservice.

Questions that could be asked during the discussion to help generate new strategies could include:

1   What is a logical next short-term goal for making these interactions more effective, and why do you think it's an appropriate choice?
2   What instructional strategies will you try, and why do you think they will work?
3   What kind of data will you bring to the next study group?
4   What is still puzzling to you? What questions do you have?

Reflections: Justify Your Teaching Strategies

To ensure that your teaching strategies are grounded in the data you analyzed and are supported by best teaching practices and learning theories, you must provide a rationale for using them. One very effective way to find support for your strategies is to consult the educational literature. In most cases, a rationale for using the strategy will accompany the description of its purpose and use. Your justification should provide an explicit link with your description of the strategy, your data, and the educational research or theories that support their use. When you become engaged in this process, you may find that your strategies are supported by your data and connected with educational theory and best practice, but only weakly. In that case, you should either try to improve your justification or find better teaching strategies. If you are not able to justify your teaching strategies, then you should reconsider whether they are appropriate for the context in which you are planning to use them. Understanding why your strategies will work is a key part of the action research process. It will inform both your teaching and your ability to design action research projects. Questions that could be asked during the discussion to generate justifications for your teaching strategies could include:

1   How does the data support the implementation of these new teaching strategies?
2   How do best practice and educational theory support the implementation of the newly designed teaching strategies?
3   What connections are there between the results of the data analysis and current best practice and educational theory?

Reflection 9.7

Provide two more example questions that could be asked during the Reflections part of the discussion.

_____

_____

How could the facilitator provide support for group members during the discussion?

_____

_____

What kind of materials could be provided during the discussion to support the facilitator and the work of the study group?

_____

_____

---

6 Summary

Effective collaboration on action research can be enhanced through the creation of teacher study groups. Considerations when forming a teacher study group are time management, group norms, and creating a format for structured conversations. Time management should address the number of meetings, when they should occur, and how long they should be. There should also be a plan outlining what type of data should be discussed at each meeting. The group norms should specify the ground rules for the working relationships within the study group. Examples of group norms could include maintaining a non-judgmental disposition, practicing professional courtesy, and using discussion skills such as pausing, paraphrasing, and probing.

Establishing a format for structured conversations can help keep the conversation focused. The format described in this chapter is based on the four-step cycle of action research emphasized throughout the book: plan, collect data, analyze, and reflect. The conversation should begin with the plan for conducting the action research project, including a description of the research question, the participants, and the sources of data. Next, the actions taken during the action research project should be described, including both teaching and action research procedures. During the third phase of the conversation, teachers examine and make observations about the data they have gathered. There should be a conscious effort to examine the data from as many different perspectives as possible. Finally, the teachers should use their observations to reflect on the data, by interpreting their observations, developing new teaching strategies, and justifying those strategies using best practice, research, and educational theory. Teachers should be aware of the types of questions that can help facilitate each phase of the discussion. In addition, designating a facilitator may help the group move through each stage of the process more efficiently.

ten

Reading and Writing Action Research

The differences in methodology between traditional research and action research are minor. Each investigator attempts to define the problem being studied with precision, to derive his hypotheses from as rich a background of information as possible, to design an inquiry so that it will result in a genuine test of the hypotheses, to use facts or evidence rather than subjective impressions throughout the research procedure, and to generalize cautiously and tentatively from the evidence collected.

(Stephen Corey, 1953, p. 143)

1 Introduction

Very early in the educational use of action research, Hunnicutt (1950) identified six characteristics of action research projects: (1) recognition of a problem; (2) planning of procedures to study the problem; (3) selection of research techniques; (4) collection of data; (5) analysis and interpretation of data; and (6) application of the findings.

The aim of this chapter is to show you how to write an action research report. The structure of a research report constitutes its own particular "genre" of writing, i.e., they have a unique structure that serves the specific purposes of the researchers. Mastering this structure will make you a better reader and writer of research reports.

Writing action research reports serves three important purposes. First, it provides a convenient summary of your work for other teachers, administrators, or parents. Second, it also provides a focus for conversations about action research. Third, the process of writing and revising the report is an excellent way to clarify and deepen your thinking. Writing an action research report could be described as recording each step of your thinking process as you worked through the problem. Paying careful attention to your thinking can help you become more focused, more objective, and more creative when interpreting data. Contrary to the initial opinions of many newcomers to research, the literacy skills associated with the reading and writing of research are much more important than the ability to utilize statistical analysis.

There is no uniform or standard format for action research reports. For some action research projects, a more informal presentation; such as a narrative summary, a Power Point presentation, or an artistic display may best serve the purposes of the researchers and the study. Our version of an action research report will be structured similarly to reports of educational research articles. We believe a more structured approach to action research best reinforces your learning of the analytical thinking processes associated with action research.

In an educational research report, it would be common to have sections entitled Purpose, Participants, Procedures, Data Collection, Findings, and Discussion. However, the names and total number of sections often vary according to the type of research. In the format presented below, we have reorganized these under the headings of Plan, Collect Data, Analyze, and Reflect. This has been done to remain consistent with the previous vocabulary in the text and also to reinforce the systematic thinking processes discussed throughout the text.

> All research reports constitute an elaborate answer to four questions. By looking for the answers to these questions as you read action research reports, you can get to the essence of the study much more quickly:
>
> 1 What was the purpose of the study?
> 2 How was the data collected and analyzed?
> 3 What did the researchers find when they collected the data?
> 4 What do the findings mean?

> Bazerman (1988) traces the emergence of research reports back to the seventeenth and eighteenth centuries to the time Newton was introducing his findings on optics.

Reflection 10.1

Read through the action research report located in Appendix A. As you read through the report, you may notice that it is blocked into sections. Every section is written in a slightly different way. Each of these sections serves a different purpose, which makes it easier for experienced readers to find information and ultimately easier to understand the study. Write down the titles of the sections you see in the example research report.

_____

_____

_____

_____

2 Plan: Purpose Section

The Plan section of an action research report contains several subsections, each of which describes a specific part of the plan. The purpose section explains the purpose for the study. The Participants and Setting section describe who took part in the study and where the study occurred, and the Sources of Data section describes the tests, interviews or survey questions, or type of assignment used to gather the data. Each of these will be explained in more detail in the sections below.

The purpose of an action research project is explicitly stated at the very beginning of the study. As part of the Purpose section, some background information and an explanation of the rationale for the study usually accompany the statement of purpose. The rationale for the study could include an explanation of why the proposed action should be effective or what outcomes you expect. When writing your own Purpose section, you may also want to talk about what interested you in the research or what drew you into the research or why this research is important to your school. Other relevant information would include the results of previous studies or the findings from other studies. In a more formal research report (like those published in research journals), a review of literature usually follows in its own section. In action research reports like the example in Appendix A, this is not considered essential.

Reflection 10.2

After you have identified a topic, it is crucial that you create an explicit statement of purpose or pose an explicitly stated research question as a central component of the Purpose section. Go to the example paper in Appendix A and write down the explicit statement of purpose or the explicitly posed research question from the purpose section.

_____

_____

_____

---

3 Plan: Participants and Setting

An important feature of all research reports is the information provided about the setting and the participants. How these are treated may vary according to the research discussed. For example, the comments of a third grade reading tutor on the guided reading program will probably carry more weight than those of the physical education instructor. It may also make a difference as to how the reader draws conclusions if she knows whether this participant has been teaching for five or fifteen years, how long she has been teaching reading, and whether or not she has a master's degree. It may also be important to know if the students are accomplished readers, how many are classified as special needs students, how many students qualify for free and reduced lunch, and perhaps what units have been previously introduced. These are just a few examples of the type of contextual factors that may be important to readers. In a similar way, educational settings are highly unique. It does matter to readers whether the study was conducted in an urban or rural school, with high or low achievers, or even at the beginning or end of the school year.

When you write up your studies, you will have to decide what information is essential for the reader. Ultimately, it is the research question, i.e., the purpose of the study that determines what contextual information is important. In order to gain a better appreciation of the crucial role a detailed description of the participants plays in understanding a research study, go to the example action research report in Appendix A.

Reflection 10.3

(a) Examine the description of the participants. Explain how the information relates to the research question.

_____

_____

_____

(b) Describe your impressions of the class described in the *Participants* section.

_____

_____

_____

(c) Change one of the key pieces of information in the description of participants and explain how those changes will influence the conclusions readers could draw from the study.

_____

_____

_____

(d) Consider the research question you wrote in Chapter 2. Who would the participants be in your action research project?

_____

_____

_____

---

4 Plan: Source of Data

After you have formulated a research question, identifying your purpose and participants, you must also describe your source of data. Sources of data in an action research project could include but are not limited to student work, artifacts of your teaching, standardized test scores, interview responses, survey results, observations, or videotapes of your teaching. These descriptions provide an important basis for the reader to appropriately evaluate the data, and hence the findings from your study.

- *Observing students* Include a description of any checklists, implementation logs, student response charts, or other instruments used in the study.
- *Observing teachers* Include a description of any checklists, implementation logs, coding schemes, or other instruments used in the study.
- *Surveys* Include a description and examples of the survey items and the type of response scale. The complete survey should be included in an appendix.
- *Interviews* Include a description and examples of the interview questions. All the interview questions should be included in an appendix.
- *Standardized achievement test* Include the name of the test and a description of the scores utilized; or the type of test items on a chapter test (essay or objective), how the score was calculated, and information needed for the reader to interpret the scores.
- *Pre- and post-tests* Include the name of test and a description of the items and the criteria used to interpret the results.

Reflection 10.4

Describe the sources of data in the example action research report in Appendix A.

_____

_____

_____

---

5 Data Collection

The Data Collection section of the action research report includes a description of the step-by-step procedures of how the study was conducted. It might include one of more of the following components:

- *Description of the Teaching Procedures* This would include a description of how the lesson was conducted. This would be important for readers to effectively judge whether or not your strategies were implemented appropriately, were effective in general or in part, and if effective only in part, which parts were effective or what component of your strategies were effective.
- *Description of Data Collection Procedure* This would include a description of how you collected the data. For example, you might describe the instructions you gave for writing an essay, explain in what part of the lesson the essay was assigned, and the length of time students had to write the essay.
- *Description of Analysis* This would include a step-by-step description of your thinking as you analyzed the data. For example, you might outline the steps of an ITBS analysis, e.g., how you arranged the data, how the data was grouped, how you graphed the data, and what specific information you considered important when drawing conclusions. Descriptions

like these are invaluable for helping readers understand your thinking and for providing models of analytical thinking for those interested in doing similar work.

Sometimes, the importance of this information can be better appreciated when we see how its absence changes the reader's interpretation of the study.

Reflection 10.5

Read the following description of data collection from an action research study that investigated the number of discipline referrals in an elementary school over a three-month period. Explain why it would be harder to draw an appropriate conclusion from the first example compared to the second. How will the additional information help the reader make a more informed decision about the research?

Example #1 The data was recorded and organized by the intervention room associate as requested by the principal. She tallied the results by category for the months of March, April, and May.

Example #2 The data consists of the number of discipline referrals that were issued by grade level. The discipline referrals were recorded and organized by the intervention room associate as requested by the principal. She sorted the infractions into categories, then tallied the number of discipline referrals by category and grade level for the months of March, April, and May. These categories included Trustworthiness, Respect, Responsibility, Fairness, Caring, and Citizenship.

_____

_____

_____

Reflection 10.6

Go to the example in Appendix A and find the description of the actions. Which of the three types of actions characterized under Data Collection on p. 153 would best describe these procedures? Briefly summarize the procedures from the example.

_____

_____

_____

---

6 Findings

The Findings section of the action research reports the results of your analysis. It is one of the most important sections in the research report. To discover the findings is why the researcher did the study. Similarly, learning about the findings is what motivates others to read the report. The Findings should be limited to the absolute facts, what anyone could agree on. There should be data for each of your measures (ITBS scores, interview or survey questions, chapter tests, etc.), and the data should directly address the research questions. This section could also be referred to as the "Results" in an educational research study.

One of the most difficult tasks for relatively inexperienced writers of research reports is to separate facts from inferences. Facts belong in the Findings section; inferences belong in the Reflection (next) section. If the findings are well organized, they will lead to the ideas expressed in the reflection section. When analyzing an interview, facts are reported regarding the comments of the participants. When analyzing a survey, facts are reported concerning the responses of the participants. When analyzing standardized achievement scores, facts are reported concerning trends or comparisons in the scores. When analyzing pre- and post-test scores, facts are reported concerning comparisons between the baseline, the pre-test, and the post-test.

Reflection 10.7

Read through the following four statements taken from the sample research report in Appendix A. The statements are organized in two pairs. In each pair, one statement is more factual (findings section) and one statement makes a more general statement about the data (reflection section). Put an "F" by the statements you think were taken from the findings section and a "R" by the statements taken from the Reflections section, i.e. put an "F" by statements of fact and an "R" by broader and more general statements.

_____ 1   Three students specifically replied that group work made the work easier.

_____ 2   First of all, we need to be educating all students; not just worrying about bringing up students who are lower ability or just advancing the students with higher ability.

_____ 3   My small group gets distracted: the average score for this question was 3.66.

_____ 4   Although there were many differences in their responses, it was very apparent that the students were in the same classroom receiving the same information; they simply processed and expressed that information in different ways.

To increase the number of your findings, examine the subject of your study from different perspectives. Changing your perspective will yield more insight by multiplying the number of observations. It will also provide more information upon which you can reflect. Below, three approaches are given to changing your perspective:

1   Teacher researchers create comparisons and contrasts in order to measure change. They compare their data to baseline data, pre-assessment data, or comparison group data, i.e., data from a group that did not receive the teaching modification.

2 Researchers examine the data through different conceptual or theoretical frames. For example, a classroom discussion can be analyzed according to the type of questions asked, the teacher's wait time, and the degree to which students can elaborate on their responses. Each of these different perspectives can provide insights that might otherwise remain hidden.

3 Researchers combine and recombine data in different groups, searching for patterns both across the entire data and within subsets of the data. Unfortunately, many novice researchers believe there is only one answer to a research question or are unwilling to make the painstaking effort it takes to carefully and systematically comb through the data. Experienced researchers, who know from experience the effort in collecting valid data and who are aware of the multiple stories that any set of data can tell, try to extract as much information from the data as they can. They may suggest several possible interpretations before stating a preferred interpretation.

Reflection 10.8

Go to the action research report example in Appendix A and find examples for each of the three types of analyses described above.

_____

_____

_____

---

7 Reflection

The part of the report that deals with reflection is distinctly different from the Findings section. The facts of the study have already been stated in the Findings, so they do not need to be restated. In the Reflection section, the researcher interprets or explains what the data means, proposes new strategies, and provides a justification for why those strategies will work. You should begin by providing a brief summary of the most important findings, but that should be followed by an extended discussion of what they mean. When drawing conclusions, you may only examine the data that you have presented to the reader. You must exclude any unstated assumptions, personal beliefs, or previous experiences. This promotes communication between reader and writer because all conclusions are limited to information available to both. An educational research report would probably refer to this section as the "Discussion" or the "Conclusion."

In the Reflection section, you tell the story, paint the picture or otherwise connect the meaning of the facts reported under observations, especially in relation to the original research question. The data rarely speaks for itself. Successfully interpreting data requires persistent thinking from differing perspectives. It is common to offer alternative explanations for the same set of data.

Your interpretation of the data should serve as a basis for developing new teaching strategies. You can enhance your search for strategies by collaborating with peers, consulting the educational literature, and participating in a professional development program. In the final part of the reflection section, you should justify the teaching strategies you have generated by drawing on your previous experience, research-based practice, and educational theory. In this section, you will integrate theory and practice into a rationale for improving your instruction.

Reflection 10.9

(a) Find the interpretation in the example paper in Appendix A and summarize it.

_____

_____

_____

(b) Find the new teaching strategies in the example paper in Appendix A and summarize them.

_____

_____

_____

Find the justification in the example paper in Appendix A and summarize it.

_____

_____

_____

---

8 Summary

In the very simplest terms, action research reports inform the reader of the purpose of the study, who was studied and where, how the data was collected and analyzed, what the researchers found, and what they think the results mean. After reading many action research reports, the thinking processes associated with reading and writing them gradually become habitual to researchers. Eventually, it becomes second nature to conceptualize the study in its simplest terms:

1   What was the purpose of the study?
2   How was the data collected and analyzed?
3   What did the researchers find when they collected the data?
4   What do the findings mean?

These fundamental questions are organized into a series of highly structured sections of writing. The advantage to this style is that it provides maximum clarity and can also serve as a well-accepted guide to thinking. Each section accomplishes a specific purpose, which makes it easier for the reader to find desired information. Locating different forms of information in different sections of the report can also help discipline the thinking of the writer/researcher. For example, separating observations and reflections into locations within your action research report provides valuable practice at distinguishing them mentally. For the action research report to be coherent, there must be a high level of agreement among the sections. For example, the research question posed in the Purpose section must be connected to the observations and reflections made later in the report. Box 10.1 shows a rough outline of the sections in an action research report.

BOX 10.1 SECTIONS IN AN ACTION RESEARCH REPORT

Plan: the plan for research consists of several sub-sections.

Purpose Includes a description of the problem, its history, its significance, and a statement of the research question.

Setting and Participants Includes a description of the place where the study took place and the people who were part of the study. The settings and participants could be divided into two different sections.

Data Source Includes a description of the research tools (interview questions, survey, standardized tests, etc.) utilized to determine change or growth.

Data Collection Includes a description of how the study was conducted, including the teaching strategy, procedures for collecting data, and the procedures for analyzing the data.

Findings Includes a description of what the researcher found. The findings consist mainly of a series of factual, objective statements.

Reflection Explains what the findings mean, how they could be used to develop new teaching strategies, and provides a rationale for using those studies.

While the description in Box 10.1 provides a reliable guideline to writing an action research report, it should be noted that the authors of such reports often alter this fundamental organization to best serve their purposes. The number, purpose, and titles of the sections may differ among action research reports. The best way to get a feel for the right time to make such adaptations is to practice writing research reports and then get feedback from a knowledgeable reader.

Appendix A
Action Research Report Example

Plan

Purpose

The purpose of this action research study was to assess the effectiveness of implementing a cooperative learning approach in a unit on the Civil War. The purpose of the lessons that utilized cooperative learning were to examine the strategic advantages, the strategies, and the strategic outcomes for each side in the Civil War. A cooperative learning approach was selected in order to address several issues with learning for this class of students. The class appears to have high social needs; many of the students are very active and have to be reminded to stop talking frequently—although some of the females are reluctant to participate and clearly prefer to work alone. Therefore, the introduction of cooperative learning may motivate some of the students by allowing them to work together. In addition, educational research indicates that cooperative learning increases student learning and has a beneficial effect on peer interactions in diverse settings. Therefore, the research question for this study is: What impact did the use of cooperative learning during a unit on the Civil War have on student learning, peer relations, and student preferences?

Setting and Participants

This study was conducted in a seventh grade social studies class in an urban middle school. Approximately 40% of the students are on the free and reduced lunch program. The student body is diverse, consisting of Caucasian, African-American, Hispanic, and Asian students. The class consists of 20 students, including 12 boys and 8 girls. Of these,

14 are Caucasian, 3 are Hispanic, and 3 are African-American. Three of these students are receiving instruction in English as a second language. Five students have IEPs (Individualized Learning Plans), and three students take medication for ADHD (Attention Deficit Hyperactivity Disorder). There is one special needs student who receives help from the resource teacher. She is a female and has very low reading comprehension and writing ability.

A majority of the class are auditory and kinesthetic learners, although a few could be considered visual learners. The class as a whole is below grade level in reading and math. Three of them are below the 20th percentile in both subject areas. However, there are two students who are released from class to participate in the gifted and talented program. These two students have extremely high ability in reading comprehension, writing ability, and their ability to reason and problem solve.

All of the students described above took a pre- and post-test, completed the survey, and were observed. Three of students were interviewed. Each represented a larger group of students in the class.

1   Jennifer is a 12-year-old, Caucasian girl. Jenifer's ITBS (Iowa Test of Basic Skills) are at the 20th percentile. Her last report card in history was a "D." She has an IEP (Individualized Education Plan) and struggles with peer relations. She was selected for an interview because she is representative of a group of girls who appear to prefer working alone.
2   Jemar is a 12-year-old African-American boy. Gradewise, he is in the "B" to "C" range with most subjects, and his last report card grade in history was a "C." His reading scores on the ITBS are in the 40th percentile. He is very social and outgoing. He represents a segment of the class that is very talkative and appears to have high social needs.
3   Justine is a 12-year-old Hispanic girl in the gifted program. Justine is a high ability student with a 3.8 GPA. Her scores on the ITBS (Iowa Test of Basic Skills) are consistently above the 80th percentile. She consistently gets "As" in history and is one of two gifted students in the program.

Sources of Data

Pre- and Post-Tests

A pre- and post-test were given for the unit on the Civil War. Ten questions on the pre- and post-tests pertained to the material learned during the cooperative learning sessions. These questions covered three areas specifically—strategic advantages of each side during the Civil War, the strategies utilized, and the outcomes of those strategies. The questions are written in a multiple choice format and are listed on pp. 167–168.

Observations

Four observations were made while students were working in cooperative groups. Each observation lasted approximately 15 minutes. Notes were taken during the observation when possible. A journal entry was recorded for each observation after the school day was over.

Surveys

The entire class responded to a survey consisting of 15 questions. Students were asked to respond to statements on a scaled response. Below is an example question with the response scale:

Group work is my favorite activity.

Strongly Agree   Agree   Disagree   Strongly Disagree.

Each of the responses was given a number (Strongly Agree = 4, Agree = 3, Disagree = 2, and Strongly Disagree = 1), which was used to calculate the mean, median, and mode. The questions were analyzed by combining them into three categories, those questions that addressed whether the student liked to work in groups, those questions that addressed how well students interacted in cooperative groups, and those questions that addressed how well students learned in groups. Comparisons were made among the mean, median, and mode among these categories. A complete list of survey questions can be found on p. 169.

Interviews

Three students were interviewed. The interview questions were organized in a semi-structured format. They addressed whether students liked working in groups, the quality of student interactions in groups, and how much students learned in groups. A complete list of questions can be found on p. 169.

Data Collection

Teaching

The cooperative learning strategy was implemented during four lessons that were part of a three-week unit on the Civil War. The learning goals that applied to cooperative learning included understanding the strategic advantages, the overall strategy for each side, and the resulting outcomes of these strategic approaches.

To accomplish these goals, the students were organized into five cooperative learning groups of four students each. In each group, three of the four students were assigned individual roles. There was a facilitator, a recorder, and a reporter. The facilitator's role was to lead the discussion and activity of the group. The groups were to use the internet, reading materials, and other resources to compile a list of strategies and strategic advantages for each side. Then the group had to address these questions and provide supporting evidence for their answers:

1   Which side had the best strategy?
2   Which side had the most advantages?
3   Which side made the best use of their resources?
4   How could each side have changed the outcomes of the war by changing of their strategy?

The recorder recorded the group's answers, and the reporter's role was to report the group's findings to the rest of the class.

The five principles of cooperative learning were incorporated into the unit in the following way:

1   *Individual accountability* Each person in the group was assigned a role to perform in the group, was responsible for participating in a follow-up class discussion, and had to take the unit test.
2   *Positive interdependence* The class had group jobs, which had to be done cooperatively.
3   *Face-to-face interaction* Students were encouraged to arrange their desks to promote face-to-face interaction.
4   *Teaching collaborative skills* The importance of peer relations and cooperation was stressed. Students were introduced to cooperative learning through a game called *Broken Circles*, and posters were put on the walls that cued students to cooperative behaviors, such as a description of the facilitator's role in leading small group discussion.
5   *Group processing* Students had a chance to reflect on their experience with cooperative learning through the surveys and interviews used as part of this action research study.

Collecting the data

A pre- and post-test was administered before and after the unit. After the post-test was given, all students were asked to complete a survey. The survey was administered the day after the test before beginning the next history unit. It took about 10 minutes to complete. In addition, three of the students were interviewed The interviews took about 15 minutes apiece and all were conducted during silent reading time.

Findings

Pre- and Post-Tests

The class averaged 8.2 out of 10 right on the post-test. This reflected a significant gain from the pre-test average of 2/10 and compared favorably with the previous year's average of 7.4 correct on the post-test. The two most missed questions were 3 and 5. Many students answered "D" for both of these questions, indicating a lack of awareness of the Northern strategy of blockading Southern ports.

Observations of Students

Three of the five groups compiled a list of strategic advantages within the first class period. They talked in a low tone, made lots of eye contact, and gave direction to the recorders as they were writing. Two of the groups were louder, with frequent bursts of laughter. The recorder seemed to be writing at a much slower pace. In one group, two of the students talked and laughed with each other, while two of the other group members talked more quietly and referred to the materials. In the other group, two students left their seats to go look out the window. Both groups had to be reminded to be quieter.

When the teacher approached these two groups she could see their list of strategic advantages was incomplete. They were having difficulty using the resources to find the information they needed. When the teacher asked them if they needed help, the two ELL students said they didn't understand the assignment. Lacking a factual foundation, both groups had difficulty answering the four higher level questions on the assignment. Their answers appeared to be unsupported opinion. Only one or two of the group members of these groups contributed to the ensuing whole class discussion.

The other three groups were more successful in creating a complete list of strategic advantages for both sides. They were split on which side had the best strategy. Two of those groups favored the North's strategic advantages, while one group favored the South. One student said, "With their advantage in population and industry, only the incompetence of the generals could have kept the North from winning the war." Defending the opposite point of view, another student said, "Even with the North's advantages in soldiers and supplies, the South did not have to win. They only had to avoid losing, and they nearly did it." However, of the four groups that completed their list, only one of the three groups could suggest plausible strategies for altering the outcomes of the Civil War. The plans for the other two groups were not consistent with the historical facts, and the students failed to provide a very convincing rationale to support their strategies.

At the end of the class period, there was a whole class discussion of the strategic advantages for both sides during the Civil War. About half of the class participated in the discussion. Regarding the question as to which side had the most resources and best strategy, many students were able to provide informed opinions and support them with factual information. There were fewer responses to the question regarding which side made the best use of their resources. However, Elise and Justine, both gifted students, argued passionately and credibly that the North's strategic use of resources would have eventually overcome any Southern military strategy.

During the discussion, there was some talking among students at inappropriate times. Some of the students had to be reminded to stop talking frequently. Three students were not able to keep their focus on the front of the room. Their attention wandered, and when called on, these students were not able to answer questions.

Survey

The survey responses were divided into three categories according to the type of question. There were five questions that ask about their preference for working in groups (questions 1, 4, 7, 10, 13), five questions that asked how their groups functioned (questions 2, 5, 8, 11, 14), and five questions that addressed how well they learned in cooperative groups (questions 3, 6, 9, 12, 15). The mean (M), media, and mode for all the questions are summarized with the survey questions on p. 169.

The survey responses indicated that students had a strong preference for working in groups. They indicated that group work was a favorite activity (M = 3.6), that they would like to spend more time in groups (M = 3.3), that they did not prefer to work alone (M = 2.1) or in pairs, (M = 2.3), and they strongly disagreed that they worked in groups too much (M = 1.2).

The student responses in regards to group functioning were mixed. They agreed that everyone in their group had a chance to participate (M = 3.1), that they understood the role they performed in their group (M = 2.8), and they disagreed with the statement that they did not participate much in their group (M = 1.8). They were split on whether the work was divided equally among group members (M = 2.4) and whether they finished their work more quickly (M = 2.4).

The students generally felt that participating in cooperative learning groups was beneficial to their learning. They felt they learned more when working in cooperative groups than when working alone (M = 2.9), that working in small groups helped them understand better (M = 2.9), that their group members helped them learn (M = 2.8), and they had more ideas working in groups (M = 2.8). They disagreed with the statement that working in small groups did not help their understanding of the subject (M = 1.5).

Interview

The interview responses were divided into three categories according to the type of question: questions that asked about their preference for groups, questions that asked how their groups functioned, and questions that addressed how well they learned in cooperative groups.

Two of the three interviewed students said they preferred working in cooperative groups. The reasons for liking cooperative groups were mixed. Jemar said he worked in a group that was mainly his friends. He liked working with his friends, although he indicated that his group didn't function as well as it could. He felt there was a little too much talking, and he wasn't sure he could trust his friends to have the right answer. Jennifer also said she liked working in groups. This was somewhat surprising since Jennifer had previously expressed a desire to work alone. She said she could understand the material better when it was explained by her classmates and that working in groups provided more variety. Justine said that she did not enjoy working in groups. Her main reason was that she felt group members did not do equal shares of work. She felt that her classmates did not talk enough, and it was unfair that they received the same grade for their group work. She said she might have liked it more if she got to work with her friends next time.

For the most part, the students said the members of their group got along well. No one argued and there was no fighting. Justine and Jemar said their groups got off task at different times. Jemar said his group joked around a little too much, and Kaitlin said her group didn't interact enough. Jemar said part of the reason they were off task is they did not know what to do. Jennifer said her group also wasn't sure how to answer the last two questions. All three participants agreed that the groups learned best when they were asking each other a lot of questions and when they were talking a lot. But sometimes they didn't talk very much, or they talked about non-school matters.

Of the three interviewees, Jennifer said her learning benefited most from cooperative learning. She said talking to other students about what they were learning helped her understanding. She also liked the fact that she could ask her classmates questions right away when she couldn't understand something. Jemar said working in groups helped him learn, but he thinks he could have learned more had his group been more on task. He said his group members helped him learn best when they stayed on task and answered the questions. His learning wasn't as great when they joked around too much. Justine was the most dissatisfied with her learning in cooperative groups. She felt she could have learned more alone. She felt groups would work best if she was put with other people or if her current group would have tried harder.

Reflections

Interpretations

Students' interviews and surveys demonstrated a clear preference for using cooperative groups, and students generally reported that their learning was improved. Student perceptions of their learning were supported by the increase in their pre-test to post-test scores. These findings suggest that a cooperative learning approach both improved student learning while addressing the social needs of students in the class. However, some student responses and teacher observations indicated that the groups were not functioning to their full potential.

Some of the difficulties with group functioning were caused by off task behavior, as revealed by the observations and interviews. For example, Jemar was distracted by his interactions with his friends. Other behaviors may have been due to not understanding what to do. In the case of the ELL students, this may have been due to language difficulties. It may also be that some of the behaviors were caused because students were not familiar enough with cooperative learning or because the classroom norms for cooperative learning had not yet been well established. In addition, students may need more instruction in their collaboration skills. There is also some evidence that students need to improve peer collaboration skills. This may also be because the task was not inherently motivating.

There was some evidence in both the small groups and the large group discussion that students were able to achieve higher-level thinking skills. Three of the five groups debated which side had the best set of strategic advantages very well, offering numerous reasons to support their positions. However, only one of the groups was able to devise an alternative strategy for altering the outcome of the Civil War. This may be due to both a lack of factual knowledge and a need for more practice with higher level thinking skills.

New Teaching Strategies

The data from this study suggests the unit on cooperative learning could be refined by incorporating additional teaching strategies for improving interactions among group members and supporting higher level thinking skills. The following strategies are intended to improve interactions among group members:

1   Add short essays on the post-assessment to encourage and assess higher-level thinking.
2   Require that each group turn in their list of Northern and Southern strategies and also write an essay that makes an argument for which side had the best strategy and that outlines a strategy that would lead to an alternative outcome.
3   Teach more collaborative skills through team-building activities. Conduct a search for team-building activities in the literature.
4   Create a new role for the fourth member of the group as observer. This person's role would be to make observations about the group processing during the group interactions.
5   Provide some time for each group to listen to the observations made by the observer and discuss the quality of the group interactions.
6   Carefully select groups so that students are not with friends who distract them.

Several strategies could also be implemented to encourage higher-level thinking. The following strategies are intended to encourage higher-level thinking.

1   Provide more support for making the initial list of strategies:
    (a) Give more cues and guidance in the questions.
    (b) Provide more feedback.
    (c) Provide a rubric and examples for written work.
2   Teach metacognitive strategies, such as goal setting, for monitoring their own work. Examine the literature on metacognition to find specific strategies.
3   Make the task more intrinsically satisfying by allowing each group to decide whether the North or South had the best strategy and let groups debate the issue with each other.
4   Provide more visual cues (such as pictures or diagrams) for ELL learners. Examine the ELL literature for additional strategies.
5   Examine the literature for more specific adaptations for individual students.

Justifications

The primary justification for the strategies to improve peer interactions in the groups comes from the five principles of cooperative learning. The five principles of cooperative learning are intended to provide a guide to organizing and structuring groups. Adding short essays on the test and requiring a group writing assignment are supported by the first two principles of cooperative learning: individual accountability and positive group interdependence. Increasing the accountability at both levels may help students stay more focused on the task and thus improve group interactions. Engaging in the writing process on both the individual and group level will also encourage higher level thinking skills, such as analysis and synthesis.

Teaching collaborative skills through team-building activities is supported by the fourth principle of cooperative learning. Engaging students in more team-building activities may help foster a classroom climate and classroom norms for cooperative learning. It may also help establish a stronger bond between students, thus leading to higher quality interactions. Finally, it may help students to see more benefit in cooperative learning.

Creating an observer role and allowing time for group processing will address the fifth principle of cooperative learning. The observer could share his or her observations of group interactions as a way of initiating a discussion about the group's interactions near the end of the unit.

The strategies to improve thinking skills are supported by three major strands of the educational literature. The first strand originated with Vygotsky's conception of the zone of proximal development. This theory suggests that students can reach higher levels of thinking with teacher assistance. Providing more support in the form of increased feedback, cues, guiding questions, rubrics, and example work may help provide more insight and strategies for students, thus reducing the downtime in groups due to a lack of understanding. The second strand is the research on metacognition. This research has shown that more able students usually possess more strategies for completing tasks and solving problems than less able students. Therefore, incorporating strategies for teaching students how to set goals and monitor their own learning in this unit may help students better recognize when they are struggling and need help from the teacher. The third strand involves encouraging thinking through writing. Language plays an important role in thinking; therefore, improvements in writing are often an indication of better thinking. In addition, writing assignments will provide the teacher with more opportunities to evaluate, diagnose, and facilitate student thinking. This approach will also provide more opportunities for ELL students to receive feedback on their writing in English; however, this will also require they are provided with more supporting instruction.

Instruments

The pre- and post-test multiple choice questions, the survey questions and the interview questions are shown here.

PRE- AND POST-TEST QUESTIONS

1   Southern advantages at the beginning of the Civil War included _____
   A)   factories for producing military supplies.
   B)   a large population for recruiting soldiers.
   C)   excellent soldiers and generals.
   D)   numerous railroads for moving troops and supplies.

2   At the beginning of the Civil War, the North was at a disadvantage because it lacked

   _____
   A)   food and money.
   B)   railroads and industry.
   C)   a large population.
   D)   a clear emotional picture of what it was fighting for.   *(Continued)*

(Continued)

3 The Union plan for fighting the Civil War included all the following strategies EXCEPT _____

    A) taking control of the Mississippi River.
    B) capturing Richmond, Virginia.
    C) fighting a defensive war.
    D) blockading Southern ports.

4 The Confederacy expected to obtain war materials and supplies from _____
    A) Europe.
    B) West Point.
    C) Canada.
    D) factories in the South.

5 The main goal of the Confederate navy was to _____
    A) do battle with ironclad ships.
    B) cut off supplies to the Northern Army of Virginia.
    C) break the Union blockade of Southern ports.
    D) commandeer tugboats, ferries, and schooners.

6 General Robert E. Lee's plans before the Battle of Antietam included all the following objectives EXCEPT _____
    A) destroying Northern morale.
    B) issuing the Emancipation Proclamation.
    C) winning British and French support.
    D) surprising Washington, D.C., from the north.

7 The Emancipation Proclamation resulted in _____
    A) freeing slaves in the border states.
    B) strengthening the Confederacy.
    C) transforming the Civil War into a fight against slavery.
    D) winning foreign powers to the side of the South.

8 Slavery was abolished in every state in the Union by the _____
    A) Battle of Antietam.
    B) surrender of Robert E. Lee.
    C) Emancipation Proclamation.
    D) Thirteenth Amendment.

9 The North turned the war in its favor with its victory at the Battle of _____
    A) the Merrimack and the Monitor.
    B) Fredericksburg.
    C) Gettysburg.
    D) Cemetery Hill.

10 Confederate troops abandoned Richmond as a result of Ulysses S. Grant's _____

    A) siege of Petersburg, Virginia.
    B) capture of Appomattox Court'House, Virginia.
    C) march to the sea.
    D) repeated attacks on Robert E. Lee's defenses at Petersburg.

Survey Questions

1 Group work is my favorite activity.
   (Mean = 3.6, Median = 4, Mode = 4)
2 The work was divided equally among group members.
   (Mean = 2.4, Median = 2, Mode = 2)
3 I learn more when working in small groups compared to working alone.
   (Mean = 2.9, Median = 3, Mode = 3)
4 I prefer to work alone.
   (Mean = 2.1, Median = 2, Mode = 2)
5 I did not participate very much in my group.
   (Mean = 1.8, Median = 2, Mode = 2)
6 My group members helped me learn.
   (Mean = 2.8, Median = 3, Mode = 3)
7 I enjoy learning more when working in groups compared to working alone.
   (Mean = 3.3, Median = 3, Mode = 3)
8 I understood the role I was assigned in the small group.
   (Mean = 2.8, Median = 2, Mode = 2)
9 I had more ideas when working in groups than when working alone.
   (Mean = 2.8, Median = 2, Mode = 2)
10 We worked in groups too much.
   (Mean = 1.2, Median = 1, Mode = 1)
11 I finish my work more quickly when working in a small group than when working alone.
   (Mean = 2.4, Median = 2, Mode = 2)
12 Working in small groups helped me understand better.
   (Mean = 2.9, Median = 2, Mode = 2)
13 I would like to spend more time in groups.
   (Mean = 3.3, Median = 3, Mode = 3)
14 Everyone in my small group has a chance to participate.
   (Mean = 3.1, Median = 3, Mode = 3)
15 Working in groups did not help my understanding of the subject.
   (Mean = 1.5, Median = 1, Mode = 1)

Interview Questions

1 Tell me about how your group worked together. (Possible follow-up questions: Give me some examples of what you mean?)
2 What did you like best about working in your group?
3 Describe how your group works when it is working well.
4 What did your group not do well?
5 What have you learned about the topic from working in small groups?
6 In what ways do you feel your group members helped you learn the material?
7 Based on this experience, do you prefer working in a group or would you rather work alone?

Appendix B
Sample Answers and Discussion Guide

Chapter 1 An Introduction to Action Research

Reflection 1.1

Answers will vary. When you have finished reading the chapter re-examine your answer and consider its correspondence with the four-step cycle of action research and/or the differences with action research. For the four-step cycle of action research, look for parts of your answer that indicate the need for planning, data collection, analysis, and reflecting. For differences with action research, look for parts of your answer that emphasize the more formal aspects of data collection and analysis, such as the use of specialized equipment or statistical analysis.

Reflection 1.3

1 qualitative
2 quantitative
3 qualitative
4 quantitative
5 quantitative

Reflection 1.4

Answers will vary, but they may include references to location of the research, the data sources, the selection of participants, and the analysis of data. Action research is usually located in schools, the participants are usually the researcher's students, the data sources are tests, classroom tests, or the analysis does not require the use of statistics or other complex analytical tools. For discussion, try to identify the parts of your answer that correspond with the four-step cycle of action research: plan, collect data, analyze, and reflect.

Reflection 1.5

1   R
2   T
3   R
4   R
5   T
6   T
7   R

Reflection 1.6

Answers will vary. For discussion, examine your teaching narrative and try to identify parts of your description that are related to planning, acting, observing, or reflecting. To what degree is your current thinking process related to the thinking associated with action research? Also discuss how refining that thinking process could be of additional benefit.

Reflection 1.7

Answers will vary. Your examples should reinforce the importance of actively considering the rights of the child, such as:

1   A videotape of a special needs child who is struggling with reading is seen at an inservice session by the child's aunt. The parents learn of the video and are distraught about the unfavorable portrayal of their child.
2   Referring to a child with a specific disability so it is obvious which student you are discussing.
3   Using the child's first name instead of a pseudonym.

Reflection 1.8

1   N
2   N
3   A
4   A

Reflection 1.9

Answers will vary. As a teacher, you have a professional obligation to protect the child from harm. Your answers should adress the need for additional protection of the child's rights when conducting action research. For discussion, take advantage of this opportunity to let teachers explore the role differences between teaching and action research.

Reflection 1.10

Answers will vary. Those who plan to limit their action research projects to improving instruction within their classroom will not need to consider a special course of action. Your ethical obligations as a teacher to protect the rights of the child will be sufficient. Those who are thinking about publishing may offer one of several approaches, including asking students and parents for their consent after the course is over, having a third party solicit consent without informing the teacher until the course is over, or doing an action research project in another teacher's class. You may also have made some suggestions for creating a consent form or gaining permission from the principal or school board.

Chapter 2   Planning an Action Research Project

Reflection 2.1

Answers will vary. However, you should have asked more than one question and preferably several questions. That would suggest that you have considered the observations from more than one perspective. The following are possible questions:

1   Is the reading level of the short story too high?
2   Are students sufficiently interested in the short stories?
3   Are students practiced in higher-level thinking skills?
4   Could I ask better questions?
5   Is there a way I could better motivate my students?
6   Is there a better way to organize the discussion?
7   Have I clearly communicated my expectations to students?

Reflection 2.2

Answers will vary. However, you should have asked more than one question and preferably several questions. That would suggest that you have considered the observations from more than one perspective. The following are possible questions:

1   Could Alicia become more independent?
2   How could Alicia become more intrinsically motivated?
3   Could the curriculum be more relevant to Alicia's interests?

Reflection 2.3

Answers will vary. However, you should have asked more than one question and preferably several questions. That would suggest that you have considered the observations from more than one perspective. The following are possible questions:

1   Are these students as proficient in English as they appear in the classroom?
2   Are these students receiving enough supporting instruction?
3   Do these students need more classroom adaptations?
4   Is there an awareness of cultural differences in the school?
5   Would the students score higher if the standardized tests were read aloud to them?

Reflection 2.4

Answers will vary. However, you should have asked more than one question and prefer-ably several questions. That would suggest that you have considered the observations from more than one perspective. The following are possible questions:

1   Do these students need more instructional guidance?
2   Are the directions given clearly enough?
3   Are the students motivated by the topic?
4   Would more direct instruction be beneficial?

Reflection 2.5

Answers will vary. However, you should have asked more than one question and prefer-ably several questions. That would suggest that you have considered the observations from more than one perspective. The following are possible questions.

1   Should different strategies be employed to teach computational math at the fourth grade level?
2   Is enough time devoted to computational math each day?
3   Are the low scores for computational math related to a developmental problem with fourth graders?

Reflection 2.6

Answers will vary. The purpose of this entire exercise is to suggest the importance of being as generative and productive in creating potential research questions as possible. You can always discard undesired questions later.

Reflection 2.7

(a) Answers will vary. Your answer should include supporting reasons for your choice of questions.
(b) Answers will vary. Possibilities might include
    1   Offer participation credit.
    2   Give a quiz over the story at the beginning of class.
    3   Try reading different stories.
    4   Build motivation by improving teacher–student relationships.
    5   Ask questions that relate the story to students' background knowledge.
    6   Ask higher-level questions.

Reflection 2.8

Answers will vary, but your answer should now include mention of a specific strategy. For example:

1 Will the use of higher level thinking questions during discussions improve the essay scores on social studies tests?
2 Will giving students a choice about the book they read improve participation during discussions?

Reflection 2.9

(a) Answers will vary. The following are possibilities:
  1 What short stories do you assign that get a positive response from students?
  2 How do you make your short stories relevant to students?
  3 How do you encourage higher level thinking in your classes?
  4 What kind of question-asking strategies do you use in your short story units?

(b) Answers will vary. Pay attention to whether your answer includes the use of data and, if so, make note of what kind of data. As you work through the book, a measure of your learning will be your ability to successfully utilize more forms of data.

Reflection 2.10

Answers will vary. Possibilities might include sessions on:

1 question-asking strategies
2 reading strategies
3 intrinsic motivation
4 reader response strategies.

Reflection 2.11

Answers will vary, but the strategies you have identified may make good starting points for action research projects. To create an action research project, design a way to evaluate the new teaching strategy, implement the strategy, then collect data, and analyze it.

Reflection 2.12

1 P
2 S
3 S
4 P
5 P
6 S

Reflection 2.13

(a) Answers will vary. This question gives you an opportunity to examine your professional reading habits. As you move through this section, try to find at least three strategies both for increasing your reading and then applying what you read to your practice.

(b) Answers will vary. You are more likely to be reading articles from secondary literature. Secondary literature is a valuable source of information and strategies. To expand your professional horizons, try to extend your expertise into primary literature. This will take much practice, and it will be helpful if you pick subjects in which you have a high interest.

Reflection 2.14

(a) You would probably have to use information you could find in free electronic databases online, such as ERIC and Google Scholar. In this case, your choices would be limited by your lack of access. You would have to depend on the full text articles you could find through these sources.

(b) In this case you could use databases provided through your university library to obtain more full text articles electronically through Education Full Text, JSTOR, or ERIC. You could also request that your university library mail you hard copies of articles not available on full text. That way you could integrate the convenience of electronic sources without sacrificing the additional information found in hard copies.

(c) In this case, you can use the resources to maximize convenience with a thorough coverage of the literature. To facilitate the speed and efficiency of your search, you could search the electronic databases to obtain a broad range of full text articles as rapidly as possible. You could examine the reference sections of these articles to find additional articles on the same topic. The reference sections usually contain widely read articles on the topic. Use those references to search for additional articles stored both electronically and in print.

Reflection 2.15

Answers will vary. Search terms should match with the topic of interest.

Reflection 2.16

Answers will vary. Answers should refer to articles that can be cited in educational journals.

Reflection 2.17

1   O
2   T
3   S or I
4   T
5   O
6   S or I

Reflection 2.18

Observations. One approach would be to compare the number of times students participate before and after the introduction of cooperative learning.

Reflection 2.19

(a) Will using cognitive strategies help Alicia complete her assignments independently of the teachers?
(b) Observations. The number of times Alicia asked for assistance before and after introducing the strategies could be compared. In addition, the quality of her work before and after could be compared.

Reflection 2.20

(a) Will speaking more slowly when giving directions, increasing the number of visual aids, and making the instruction more relevant increase the standardized test scores of Hispanic students?
(b) Test scores. Improving learning as measured by test scores is the purpose of the research.

Reflection 2.21

(a) Will providing rubrics, exemplars from previous classes, and the setting of short term goals help students finish their work on time for the inquiry-based science unit?
(b) Observations. This could best be determined by examining student work for timeliness and quality.

Reflection 2.22

(a) Will introducing a daily practice problem to fourth graders increase their standardized achievement test scores?
(b) Test scores. Improving learning as measured by test scores is the purpose of the research.

Chapter 3 Observing Students and Their Work

Reflection 3.1

(a) Each has a different phrase written within the triangle.
(b) The triangles are the same size. Each phrase has five words. Each phrase has a repeated word.
(c) "THE," "A," and "THE."
(d) Often we don't notice details because we don't expect to see them. What you see is influenced by what you expect to see.
(e) Action researchers must make a careful effort to systematically observe so their assumptions don't cause them to miss key elements.

Reflection 3.2

(a) The two pictures contain intersecting lines that are perpendicular to each other. The picture on the left is about twice as large as the one on the right.
(b) Answers may vary, but many people would say they see two telephone poles, one farther away than the other.
(c) Your assumptions can influence what you see. Therefore, it is always important for researchers to try to be aware of their assumptions and to try to temporarily suspend their biases.

Reflection 3.3

Research questions will vary. They should be stated in the form of a question and should provide a specific focus for the investigation.

Reflection 3.4

(a) Answers will vary. The description of the problem space should include a consistent time and location for the observations. The problem space should be relevant to the research question asked in (b), i.e., it should be clear that making observations in the problem space could lead to an answer to the research question.
(b) Answers will vary. Answers that refer to students should include information related to their grade level, ability level, ethnicity, gender, special needs, and other relevant information. For teachers, a description might include their subject area, years of experience, level of education and other information relevant to the research question.

Reflection 3.5

Answers will vary. They may include the use of audio or videotapes, journaling, or note taking.

Reflection 3.6

Answers will vary, but they should contain a significant level of detail and reflect an effort to observe in a systematic fashion.

Reflection 3.7

The three groups on task successfully completed a list of strategic advantages and made an argument for which side made the best use of their resources. Only one of the three groups could suggest a plausible alternative strategy. The two groups off task had difficulty completing this part of the assignment.

Reflection 3.8

Two groups were off task. These two groups were also not able to successfully complete their work. The two ELL students appeared not to understand how to complete the assignment. Some of the students in the off task group appeared to be working.

Reflection 3.9

Both groups had trouble addressing the higher level questions. Their answers appeared to be unsupported opinion. Only one of the four groups could suggest plausible strategies for altering the outcome of the Civil War. The strategies of other groups were not consistent with the historical facts, and the students failed to provide a very convincing rationale to support their strategies. During discussion, many students were able to provide informed opinions and support them with historical facts.

Reflection 3.10

The groups that were off task did not achieve higher-level thinking.
Two of the groups that were on task achieved some higher-level thinking but not all.
One group achieved all the higher-level thinking skills.

Reflection 3.11

Answers will vary, but the following are several possible explanations.

1 Students were organized into homogeneous groups, thus the high ability and low ability students were grouped together.
2 The ELL students may have needed more support.
3 Off task behaviors may have kept some students from reaching the higher-level thinking skills.
4 The level of thinking was so challenging that students tried to avoid the problem by engaging in off task behavior.

Reflection 3.12

The data from this study suggests the unit on cooperative learning could be refined by incorporating additional teaching strategies for improving interactions among group members and supporting higher level thinking skills. The following strategies are intended to improve interactions among group members:

1 Add short essays on the post-assessment to encourage and assess higher level thinking.
2 Require that each group turn in their list of Northern and Southern strategies and also write an essay that makes an argument for which side had the best strategy and that outlines a strategy that would lead to an alternative outcome.
3 Teach more collaborative skills through team-building activities. Conduct a search for team-building activities in the literature.
4 Create a new role for the fourth member of the group as observer. This person's role would be to make observations about the group processing during the group interactions.
5 Provide some time for each group to listen to the observations made by the observer and discuss the quality of the group interactions.
6 Carefully select groups so that students are not with friends who distract them.

Several strategies could also be implemented to encourage higher level thinking. The following strategies are intended to encourage higher-level thinking.

1 Provide more support for making the initial list of strategies.
   (a) Give more cues and guidance in the questions.
   (b) Provide more feedback.
   (c) Provide a rubric and examples for written work.
2 Teach metacognitive strategies, such as goal setting, for monitoring their own work. Conduct a literature search to find specific strategies.
3 Make the task more intrinsically satisfying by allowing each group to decide whether the North or South had the best strategy and let groups debate the issue with each other.

Reflection 3.13

The primary justification for the strategies to improve peer interactions in the groups comes from the five principles of cooperative learning. The five principles of cooperative learning are intended to provide a guide to organizing and structuring groups. Adding short essays on the test and requiring a group writing assignment are supported by the first two principles of cooperative learning: individual accountability and positive group interdependence. Increasing the accountability at both levels may help students stay more focused on the task and thus improve group interactions. Engaging in the writing process on both the individual and group level will also encourage higher level thinking skills, such as analysis and synthesis.

Teaching collaborative skills through team-building activities is supported by the fourth principle of cooperative learning. Engaging students in more team-building activities may help foster a classroom climate and classroom norms for cooperative learning. It may also help establish a stronger bond between students, thus leading to higher quality interactions. Finally, it may help students see more benefit in cooperative learning. The fifth principle of cooperative learning will be addressed by creating an observer role and allowing time for group processing. The observer could share his or her observations of group interactions as a way of initiating a discussion about the group's interactions near the end of the unit.

Providing more support for student thinking is supported by Vygotsky's conception of the zone of proximal development. This theory suggests that students can reach higher levels of thinking with teacher assistance. Providing more support in the form of increased feedback, cues, guiding questions, rubrics, and example work may help provide more insight and strategies for students, thus reducing the down time in groups due to a lack of understanding. In addition, incorporating strategies for teaching students how to set goals and monitor their own learning may help them better recognize when they are struggling and need help.

Higher-level thinking can also be encouraged through the writing assignments. Language plays an important role in thinking; therefore, improvements in writing are often an indication of better thinking.

Reflection 3.14

Answers will vary. For discussion, compare and contrast the checklists developed by different teachers.

Reflection 3.15

(a)

1   The paper is organized around a main idea.
2   Reasons are given to support the main idea.
3   The author expresses an interesting point of view.

4   There are several spelling errors, including "univers" and "meby."
5   There are few reasons given to support the thesis.
6   There is a lack of factual information.
7   There is a lack of continuity.
8   The reasoning is faulty, e.g., "If we can live on this planet, then there must be something like it with other life forms on it too."

(b) This student appears to be lacking in factual information about the solar system. There is very little evidence of a scientific vocabulary or any knowledge base about the solar system. In addition, there is some evidence of difficulties with writing, including problems with continuity and spelling.

Reflection 3.16

(a) In comparison to the first example, the second example
1   Contains more factual information.
2   Contains more scientific vocabulary.
3   Contains more evidence of scientific reasoning.
4   The continuity in the writing is better.
5   There are no spelling errors.

(b) The second student has more scientific knowledge and is a more skilled writer than the first student. Therefore, the first student will require instructional strategies that will help him improve his spelling, his vocabulary, his continuity, and his supporting reasons.

Reflection 3.17

Contrasting the two examples can help you develop a better idea of how students develop in their writing, inform your expectations for both high and low ability writers, and provide insight into new strategies for improving writing.

Reflection 3.18

In comparison to the first excerpt, the second demonstrates increased content knowledge and associated thinking skills. For instance, Chuck uses more mathematical terms than the first example (cubes, centimeters, volume, surface area, prism), displays his ability to calculate volume and surface area, and uses mathematical reasoning to justify his choice of a cube for his package. ("I chose a cube because they have a really small surface area.")

Reflection 3.19

1   6 teacher turns.
2   138 words spoken by the teacher.
3   23 average words spoken by the teacher per turn.
4   5 student turns.
5   53 words spoken by the student.

6   10.6 average words spoken by the teacher per turn.
7   2.6–1 ratio of teacher to student words.

Reflection 3.20

1   6 teacher turns.
2   56 words spoken by the teacher.
3   9.3 average words spoken by the teacher per turn.
4   5 student turns.
5   360 words spoken by the students.
6   72 average words spoken by the teacher per turn.
7   6.4–1 ratio of student to teacher words.

Reflection 3.21

(a) In the first example, the teacher does more talking (138 total words to 53) and has a higher ratio of teacher to student talk (2.6–1). In contrast, the student talks 6.4 times as much as the teacher in the second example. Therefore, the second example has a much higher proportion of student talk than the first example.
(b) The second example is a more open, student-centered discussion. Since these examples are taken from the same teacher in the same classroom, the difference may be explained by the different purposes the teacher had for both discussions. In the first example, the teacher is providing more guidance and support because she has just introduced new mathematical concepts. In the second example the students are using their previous knowledge and are therefore able to elaborate more.

Reflection 3.22

To increase the amount of student elaboration in the first example, the teacher could provide more information and preparation time before the discussion, give the students a chance to talk in small groups before the discussion, engage the students in related activity before the discussion, ask more open-ended questions, provide more wait time, or ask more probing questions.

Reflection 3.23

These strategies are justified by the data analysis that shows less student participation than the second example. The strategies listed in the answer for Reflection 3.22 are supported by the research literature on teacher and student discourse.

Reflection 3.24

(a) Sample Observation

1   Students # 2, 3, 5, 7, 8, 16, 17, & 20 had no interactions with anyone.
2   Six students interacted with other students.
3   There were interactions between 7 girls and the teacher.
4   There were interactions between 4 boys and the teacher.
5   Most interactions occurred with students in the front and center of the class.

(b) The two high ability students are also participating in class.
(c) Neither the African-American or Hispanic students are participating, except for Justine, who is a gifted Latino student.
(d) A majority of students did not participate. The teacher focuses on students in the front and center of the room. Girls and gifted students are more likely to speak. Minority students are not speaking very much, perhaps because the teacher is not offering enough encouragement.

Reflection 3.25

To stimulate student participation, the teacher could choose more interesting topics, prepare the students more before the discussion through work in small groups or activities. To increase student-to-student interactions, the teacher could provide more wait time, encourage students to comment on the contributions of others, and teach students to ask questions of each other. To encourage more participation by African-American and Hispanic children, the teacher could direct more questions to them, choose culturally relevant topics, provide more contextualized activities related to the topic, and use cooperative learning strategies.

Reflection 3.26

The strategies described in Reflection 3.25 are part of the research literature for improving teacher and student interactions. Preparing students before the discussion should increase their ability to elaborate. Increasing wait time and teaching students question asking strategies can increase student-to-student interactions. Culturally relevant teaching has been shown to improve the performance of minority students.

Chapter 4 Observing Teachers

Reflection 4.1

Answers will vary. For discussion, you may want to try watching a video with a group of teachers. Give them the teacher's expectations, and then let them record the observations, make their interpretations, and develop new teaching strategies. You may want to work in small groups and then follow with a whole group discussion.

Reflection 4.2

60 Tallies.

Reflections 4.3–4.4

Answers will vary. For discussion, try the strategy described above in Reflection 4.1.

Reflection 4.5

Teacher B. Answers will vary, but Teacher B can add to her teaching strategies by searching the literature. Possible search terms could include direct instruction, discussion-based teaching, cooperative learning, and cooperative learning.

Reflection 4.6

Answers will vary. For discussion, compare and contrast the checklists of different teachers.

Reflection 4.7

1   knowledge
2   evaluation
3   knowledge
4   synthesis
5   knowledge
6   comprehension

Reflection 4.8

1   focus question
2   repetition
3   probing question
4   rejection
5   confirmation
6   repetition
7   elaboration
8   probing question
9   cue
10 confirmation
11 reformulation
12 confirmation

Reflection 4.9

(a) The first transcript clearly has a much higher ratio of student to teacher talk compared to the second. In addition, the teacher asks very few questions and avoids making evaluative comments (letting the student know their comment was right or wrong). The students elaborate more in the first transcript, but they use very few mathematical concepts. In the second transcript, the teacher provides more guidance to the discussion. She asks more questions, she gives evaluative responses, and she provides additional information and guidance through her follow-up responses. The student responses are shorter, but they contain more mathematical concepts and vocabulary.

(b) Answers may vary. Some sample answers include:
1   Ask more open-ended questions.
2   Ask students to explain or justify their answers (probing questions).
3   Increase wait time.
4   Give students a chance to talk in small groups before the discussion.

Chapter 5 Using Surveys in Action Research

Reflection 5.1

This question is intended to stimulate your thinking regarding what kind of problems could be addressed by survey research. Any answer that explores the perceptions of the participants would be acceptable. The following are some areas from which you could formulate questions:

1   Related to climate issues
2   Related to implementation issues
3   Related to professional development needs
4   Related to community concerns
5   Related to student concerns
6   Related to existing programs
7   Related to classroom strategies
8   Related to school services

Reflection 5.2

(a) Again, there will be a variety of answers as this question is intended to give you practice with developing your own research questions. The most important element to this answer is that you ask a question for which survey questions could be developed. It is important that you do not confuse a question written for a survey with a research question. A research question is much broader than a single question written for a survey.
   Examples of research questions:

1   What types of students are most likely to complete homework consistently?
2   What dispositions are associated with homework completers?
3   What strategies are employed by homework completers?

(b) Answers will vary. The purpose of this question is simply to stimulate your thinking about the wide variety of research topics that are available for study. Two more examples are provided below:

1   How much and what kind of preparation is needed to serve as a grade level team leader at the elementary level?
2   To what degree do middle school math teachers feel they are implementing the new curriculum?

Reflection 5.3

This question is intended to illustrate the necessity for maintaining consistency across the study. The examples below are consistent with the example research questions in the answer key for Reflection 5.2.

1   The survey would consist of elementary team leaders across the district.
2   The survey would be given to all teachers of math at the middle school level.

Reflection 5.4

Format for Research Questions 1 and 2:
   Again this question is intended to help you develop consistency in your thinking across the study. The answers below should be consistent with the research questions above.
   For the survey concerning the preparation of grade level team leaders at the elementary level, the format would be open- and close-ended. Closed questions would ask

about demographic data, such as their years of experience and whether or not team leaders had a masters degree. Open-ended questions would invite the elementary team leaders to list other experiences, both educational and personal, that helped them prepare for becoming team leaders. For the survey concerning the implementation of a new math curriculum, the format would be primarily close-ended. Math teachers would be asked closed questions about the level of implementation of specific strategies recommended by the school district.

Reflection 5.5

Open-ended Questions Sample answers

1   Please list any experiences outside of school or your educational background that helped prepare you for becoming a team leader.
2   What strategies best reflect your beliefs about teaching math?

Reflection 5.6

Scaled Responses Sample answers

1   Indicate how often you use the problem of the day.
     A. Never   B. Once a week   C. Twice a week   D. Three or more times per week
2   The problem of the day has been an effective strategy for my students.
     A. Strongly Agree   B. Agree   C. Disagree   D. Strongly Disagree

Reflection 5.7

Rating Scales Sample answers

1   Rate the average degree of difficulty for the problem of the day, with 1 being very easy and 5 being very difficult.
     1   2   3   4   5
2   Rate the amount of effort you put into solving the problem of the day, with 1 being very little effort and 5 being a very high amount of effort.
     1   2   3   4   5

Reflection 5.8

1   "Kids with Good Homework Habits Get Better Grades" This is not a good choice for a title because respondents will likely be swayed either positively or negatively by seeing that good habits equal good grades and make their responses accordingly.
2   "Homework Study" This is an effective title because it is neutral and unlikely to sway participants one way or another in their responses.
3   "What's Your Homework Style?" This is also a good title because it is neutral and one that may elicit the participants' interest.
4   "How Homework Habits Affect Grades" This title should be avoided because the association with good grades influence the responses of the participants.

Reflection 5.9

Frequency of students who did more than two hours of homework each night.

1   The mode is 9.
    6 ninth graders did more than two hours of homework per night compared to
    5 tenth graders
    2 eleventh graders
    2 twelfth graders

2   The median is in the tenth grade (8th score is the middle score).
3   The mean equals 150/15 = 10.

Frequency of students who did 1–2 hours of homework each night.

4   The mode is 11th grade.
    15 eleventh graders compared to
    9 ninth graders
    14 tenth graders
    5 twelfth graders

5   The median is in the tenth grade (22nd score out of 43)
6   The mean equals 446/43 = 10.4.

Frequency of students who did 30–59 minutes of homework each night.

7   The mode is 11th grade.
    8 eleventh graders compared to
    4 ninth graders
    7 tenth graders
    5 twelfth graders

8   The median is the 11th grade score (average of 12th and 13th score out of 24).
9   The mean equals 254/24 = 10.6.

Frequency of students who did less than 30 minutes of homework each night.

10   The mode is 12th grade.

     9 twelfth graders compared to
     4 eleventh graders
     2 tenth graders
     1 ninth grader

11   The median score is twelfth grade (average of 8th and 9th scores out of 16).
12   The mean equals 181/16 = 11.3.

Frequency of students who never did any homework each night.

13   The mode is 12th grade.

     5 twelfth graders compared to
     1 tenth grader
     2 ninth graders

14   The median score was twelfth grade (average of 4th and 5th scores out of 8).
15   The mean equals 88/8 = 11.

Reflection 5.10

TABLE 5.2 A comparison of frequency of homework among high school students

Frequency of homework	Number of 9th graders	Number of 10th graders	Number of 11th graders	Number of 12th graders
More than 2 hrs each night	6 27%	5 17%	2 7%	2 7%
1–2 hrs each night	9 41%	14 47%	15 52%	6 21%
30–59 min each night	4 18%	8 27%	8 28%	5 18%
less than 30 minutes each night	1 5%	2 7%	4 19%	9 32%
Never	2 9%	1 3%	0 0%	6 21%
Total	22 100%	30 101%	29 101%	28 99%

Reflection 5.11

1   68%
2   64%
3   59%
4   28%
5   14%
6   10%
7   14%
8   53%
9   14% (15/109)
10   40% (44/109)
11   23% (25/109)
12   15% (16/109)
13   8% (9/109)

Reflection 5.12

(a)

1   Ninth graders spend more time doing homework because they have not yet constructed enough study skills.
2   Tenth and eleventh graders spend less time doing homework because they have acquired more study skills.
3   Twelfth graders do less homework because they are not motivated.
4   Twelfth graders do less homework because they are not offered enough challenging courses.

(b) Possible strategies

1   Introduce a study skills program for ninth graders.
2   Develop a peer tutoring program so upper class students can share their study strategies.
3   Offer more choices for twelfth graders, including distance classes and courses at local colleges.

(c) Justification
     Developing a study skills program for ninth graders is supported by the data, by past experiences with the transition from eighth to ninth grade, and by the educational literature discussing the transition from middle to high school. Offering more choices and a more challenging curriculum to twelfth graders is supported by the data and consistent with the literature on reform-based high schools.

Chapter 6 Using Interviews in Action Research

Reflection 6.1

Answers will vary as this question is intended to give teachers practice with developing their own research questions. The most important element to this answer is that you ask a question for which interview questions could be developed. It is important that the reader does not substitute an interview question for a research question. This question should be broad and in many cases should indicate the perceptions of the participants are important. The answer should also indicate whether the interview will be structured or semi-structured. Two example answers are shown below.

   Research question:

How well do teachers feel they are prepared to serve on the building problem-solving team?

Interview Type: Semi-structured interview. This will enable me to begin with some open-ended questions about teachers' beliefs followed by more structured and specific questions about their classroom methods.

Reflection 6.2

Research question: To what degree are teacher's beliefs about constructivism aligned with their classroom practices?

Interview Type: Semi-structured interview. This will enable me to begin with some open-ended questions about teachers' beliefs followed by more structured and specific questions about their classroom methods.

Reflection 6.3

(a) This answer should give a rationale for selecting the participants that is consistent with the research question. For example, for a study concerning the relationship between teachers beliefs on constructivism and their methods, the researcher may want to select participants who differ in their methods. This could enable an interesting comparison. For a study regarding whether teachers feel prepared to teach on the building's problem solving team, researchers may want to select participants who have served in the past, who are currently serving, and who have been recently selected to serve. Again, this could make for interesting comparisons. Primarily, the justification should address the research question in some way.

(b) Again, the rationale should address the research question. For example, the reader may say that the participants should be representative of certain groups in the community, such as SES, ethnicity, or level of education. They may also suggest that participants may represent different relationships to the child, such as parent, grandparent, or a community member without children in school. They may also say the participants would be chosen regarding the level of awareness or reaction. For example, is the researcher looking for a significant understanding of the program or just an awareness of its existence.

Reflection 6.4

1   S
2   U
3   S
4   U
5   U
6   S

Reflection 6.5

Answers may vary, but in general they should remain consistent with the research question: "What are the biggest frustrations experienced at school for middle school students?" Three examples are given below.

1   Do you feel your classmates treat you with respect?
2   Do you feel teachers treat you with respect?
3   Do you receive adequate instruction/work time?

(b) "What do you do for fun and entertainment?" is probably the most off topic.

Reflection 6.6

Answers will vary. Below are four examples.

1   What do you know about the computerized grading system used by the school district?
2   Have you found the computerized grading system to be useful?
3   Do you feel confident that grades are reported accurately?
4   What are some of the benefits you see with a computerized grading system?

Reflection 6.7

(a) The experienced teacher and principal both note that NCLB has promoted an increased emphasis on analyzing student achievement data, and both are concerned about the potential negative effects of NCLB.

The experienced teacher and the new teacher both note that increased collaboration has been a benefit.

(b) The principal sees analysis of student achievement data as a way to improve student achievement. The teachers tend to worry more about the impact on the psyche of students.

The new teacher appears to lack enough experience to share any views with the principal.

(c) *Collaboration*—the experienced teacher says collaboration has helped her learn better communication, teaching, and assessment strategies.

Accountability—the principle discusses accountability from the perspective of promoting change and the teacher discusses the lack of financial support that has come with increased accountability.

Changes in Practice—the experienced teacher spends more time talking about student achievement data, teaching test strategies, but finds there is less time for Social Studies, and enrichment activities like art and music.

Reflection 6.8

(a)
1   Principals need to be aware of the stress caused by the rapid rate of change induced by NCLB and may need to find ways to alleviate the pressure felt by teachers.
2   Teachers may benefit from strategies for integrating art and music into the math and reading curriculum.

(b) Teacher Education programs should be encouraged to prepare preservice teachers for collaborative data analysis.

Chapter 7 Standardized Test Analysis

Reflection 7.1

(a) Areas which are below the 40th percentile and which therefore require remedial instruction: Concepts and Estimation, Science, Reference and Materials

Areas which are above the 80th percentile and which therefore indicate mastery or enrichment: Vocabulary, Reading Total, Spelling, Punctuation, Usage and Expression, Language Total

(b) Strengths: Vocabulary, Reading Total Comprehension, Spelling, Punctuation, Usage and Expression, Language Total, Problem Solving and Interpretation

Weaknesses: Reference and materials

(c) This student might benefit from individualized instruction in Concepts and Estimation, Science, Reference and Materials.

(d) This student might be a good peer tutor in the areas of Vocabulary, Spelling, and Punctuation, and Reading

Reflection 7.2

Research questions will vary. They should be stated in the form of a question, should refer to individual students, and should provide a specific focus for the investigation.

Reflection 7.3

(a) *4th grade* – Vocabulary, Comprehension, Reading Total, Word Analysis, Usage and Expression, Language Total, Concepts and Estimation, Problem Solving and Interpretation, Mathematics Total

6th grade – Word Analysis, Usage and Expression, Language Total, Concepts and Estimation, Problem Solving and Interpretation, Mathematics Total

8th grade – Word analysis, Usage and Expression, Concepts and Estimation

(b) In all three grades, maps, diagrams, reference materials and sources of information have the highest totals and have the only scores over the 80th percentile.

In eighth grade, computation and science are in the 60th percentile.

Reflection 7.4

The areas identified as needing improvement should be used as a basis for developing new strategies. At the fourth grade level, students are experiencing widespread difficulty in language and math. This may require a broader based effort in the form of a long term professional development program in one or both of these areas. At the sixth and eighth grade levels, professional development may be more targeted at the identified areas. The educational literature should also be consulted in these areas.

Reflection 7.5

Research questions will vary. They should be stated in the form of a question, should refer to a group of students, and should provide a specific focus for the investigation.

Reflection 7.6

Caucasian students

98, 95, 91, 89, 87, 83, 76, 72, 67, 65, 61, 56, 55, 55, 49, 45, 42, 34, 25, 18

African-American students

82, 67, 56, 51, 45, 45, 45, 31, 25, 15

Asian students

92, 89, 82, 80, 65, 56

Reflection 7.7

(a) Above the 80th percentile = 30%
Between 40 and 80th percentile = 55%
Below 40th percentile = 15%

(b) Above the 80th percentile = 10%
Between 40 and 80th percentile = 60%
Below 40th percentile = 30%

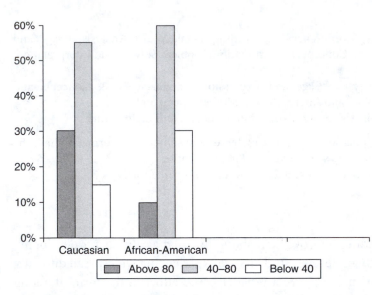

FIGURE A7.1 Comparison of Caucasian and African-American students

Reflection 7.8

(a) Caucasian students are performing at a higher level of proficiency than African-American students. This may be due to individual differences, to inequities in instruction, or to differences in socioeconomic status.

(b) Teachers could be more aware of teaching strategies to make their teaching culturally congruent with African-American students. There could be an audit of course offerings to make sure both groups were being served equally. Research on closing the achievement gap could be consulted.

(c) Strategies that promote culturally congruent teaching are justified because of the research base that has demonstrated their effectiveness for addressing the achievement gap. In this case the standardized achievement test data also supports the need for using culturally congruent teaching strategies.

Reflection 7.9

Research questions will vary. They should be stated in the form of a question, should refer to subgroups of students, and should provide a specific focus for the investigation.

Reflection 7.10

Year 2006

1   91, 90, 86, 82, 78, 72, 68, 68, 67, 59, 55, 50, 48, 45, 34, 33, 30, 26, 22, 10,
     Year 2007
2   96, 94, 87, 82, 81, 75, 73, 66, 65, 61, 57, 38, 34, 33, 32, 28, 22, 22, 19, 16,
     Year 2008

3   95, 92, 87, 85, 84, 80, 75, 73, 67, 65, 61, 58, 56, 56, 55, 51, 47, 45, 43, 21
4   *Median for 2006*   (59+55) = 114/2 = 57
5   *Median for 2007*   61+57 = 118/2 = 59
6   *Median for 2008*   65+61 = 126/2 = 63

(a) The scores are getting better. They appear to be working based on three years of standard-ized achievement data.
(b) The increase in the standardized test scores over the past three years suggests the guided reading program has had a positive impact.

Reflection 7.11

Research questions will vary. They should be stated in the form of a question, should refer to subgroups of students, and should provide a specific focus for the investigation.

Reflection 7.12

(a)

TABLE A7.1 Composite reading scores over a 3-year period for African-American students

	Above 80	40–79	Below 40
2004	10%	60%	30%
2005	20%	70%	10%
2006	10%	80%	10%

(b) The number of African-American students below the 40th percentile is decreasing. The number between 40–79th percentile is increasing. The number above the 80th percentile is relatively unchanged.

Reflection 7.13

The current strategies for addressing the needs of lower end students have been effective and should be continued. It may also be helpful to consider some additional strategies for those students who have not yet attained proficiency. Additional strategies should also be considered to push more students above the 80th percentile or the mastery level.

Reflection 7.14

(a) H(92, 3.1), C(85, 3.4), I(72, 3.3), B(66, 3.1), G(61, 2.2), E(51, 3.0), F(48, 2.9), D(42, 2.5), A(12, 1.7)
(b) Overall, there is a correlation between the percentile rank and the grade.
(c) In general, this suggests that students are performing according to their abilities.
(d) Two students, H and G, appear to be underachieving.
(e) If the students who are underachieving for the ability are African-Americans, then school officials and teachers may want to examine their equity practice in their school (e.g., see Killion, 2002) or search for new teaching strategies that specifically target African-American students.

Reflection 7.15

Research questions will vary. They should be stated in the form of a question, should refer to a relationship between data sources, and should provide a specific focus for the investigation.

Chapter 8 Pre- and Post-Tests

Reflection 8.1

On average, the students successfully achieved the learning goals for this unit.

Reflection 8.2

The improvement was not that significant. The students were highly knowledgeable on the topic before starting the unit. The learning goals were probably not appropriate or challenging enough.

Reflection 8.3

In this case, the students made a sizeable gain from the pre to post-test. The learning goals were appropriate and achieved by most students.

Reflection 8.4

(a) The group in the second year made greater gains in their learning because they knew less when they began.
(b) Again, the group in the second year appeared to learn more because their pre-test scores were the same as the first year's students, but they scored ten points higher on the post-test.
(c) Each class of students gained about 50 points from the pre to post-test. So while the third class scored higher than the first two, the gains in learning were similar.

Reflection 8.5

See Figure 8.1 opposite.

Reflection 8.6

(a) Subgroup A scored higher on both the pre- and post-test than the whole class and Subgroup B. Subgroup B scored lower than Subgroup A and the class. In addition, their rate of gain as shown on the graph was somewhat lower than those two groups.
(b) Subgroup A would probably benefit from enrichment activities. Students in Subgroup B may benefit from individual adaptations or strategies that address their particular subgroup. For example, if Subgroup B consisted of ELL students, more strategies targeting that particular subgroup should be introduced.

Reflection 8.7

(b) The adaptation worked extremely well for the first student who made dramatic gains in relation to the rest of the class. The adaptation did not work as well for the second student who did not learn at the same rate as the rest of the class.

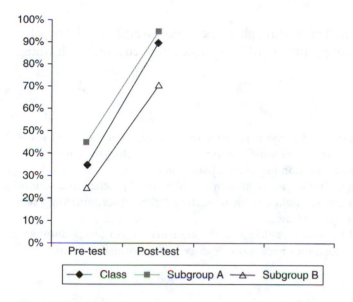

FIGURE A8.1 Pre-test post-test scores comparing subgroups to the whole class

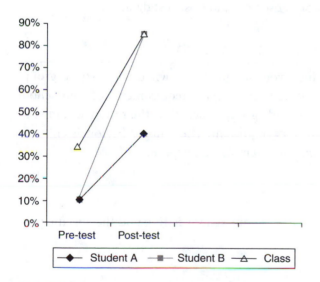

FIGURE A8.2 Pre-test post-test scores comparing individuals to the whole class

Reflection 8.8

The comparison to the baseline suggests that cooperative learning was an effective innovation. Although further comparisons need to be made, this initial study suggests that cooperative learning should be retained as a strategy. The gain in learning from pre- to post-test suggests that cooperative learning was an effective strategy.

Reflection 8.9

The causes of the Civil War were taught through cooperative learning. Thus, the gains from pre to post-test on the causes of the Civil War suggest that cooperative learning was a successful strategy.

Reflection 8.10

(a) The correct answer to the question is homonym. Based on an analysis of their answers, it appears that students do not have a good understanding the terms antonym, synonym, or homonym. Fewer students mistook a homonym for a pallidrome.
(b) Use more examples of antonym, synonym, or homonym. Give more practice in discriminating between them. The exercise could consist of sorting tasks, discriminating them during a reading task, or writing about them.
(c) These strategies are justified because it is clear that the students are confusing antonym, synonym, or homonym. Therefore, they need more practice at discriminating them.

Reflection 8.11

Research questions will vary. They should be stated in the form of a question and should provide a specific focus for the investigation. For discussion, ask students to describe possible participants and how they would use pre- and post-test data.

Chapter 9 Collaborating on Action Research

The purpose of this chapter is to help you design your own teacher study group. Consequently, answers will vary according to the specific requirements of your school setting and the purpose of your teacher study group. Therefore, the rationale and supporting reasons for your responses are very important. They should be consistent with the requirements of their school setting and their stated purpose.

Reflection 9.1

Answers will vary to suit the specific needs of your school setting and the specific purposes of your teacher study group.

Reflection 9.2

Answers will vary according to the specific purposes of your teacher study group and the time available.

Reflection 9.3

(a) Answers will vary according to the grade level of the teacher, the school setting, and other contextual factors.
(b) Your justification for the data sources should indicate that the type of research chosen is consistent with the purpose of the teacher study.

Reflections 9.4, 9.5, 9.6

Answers will vary. The example questions may be adapted to specifically address the data sources chosen by the group. They should be consistent with the description of the discussion (e.g., plan, data collection, or analysis).

Reflection 9.7

(a) Answers will vary. The example questions may be adapted to specifically address the data sources chosen by the group. They should appropriately match the description of the reflection part of the discussion.

(b) The facilitator could assist the group by
   * asking questions;
   * modeling discussion skills;
   * challenging group members to think more deeply;
   * providing support for group members;
   * creating an agenda;
   * keeping group focused and on task;
   * practicing effective time management;
   * scheduling and announce meetings.

(c) Materials created to support the group could include:
   * a year-long plan for collaborative discussions;
   * an outline of the discussion structure;
   * specific agendas for the meetings;
   * a list of example questions to ask (to promote discussion skills);
   * a form or forms to record results of the discussion;
   * a data recording sheet.

Chapter 10   Reading and Writing Action Research

Reflection 10.1

Plan

   * Purpose
   * Setting and Participants
   * Sources of Data

Data Collection

   * Teaching
   * Data Collection

Findings

   * Pre- and Post-Tests
   * Observations of Students
   * Survey
   * Interview

Reflections

- Interpretations
- New Teaching Strategies
- Justifications

Appendix

Reflection 10.2

The purpose of this action research study was to assess the effectiveness of implementing a cooperative learning approach in a unit on the Civil War.

Reflection 10.3

(a) The information about the participants can provide insight into how cooperative learning worked in this particular class. For instance, it is helpful to know that the student who complained the work was not divided equally was a gifted students. It is helpful to know that two of the students who appeared not to understand were ELL students. Knowing these details about the participants can help you draw better conclusions.

(b) The school is in an urban area, is diverse, and contains a significant minority population.

(c) Answers will vary. For discussion, explore the connections between any change in the participants and the outcomes of the research, for example if the study took place in a rural rather than an urban school. Simply trying to anticipate the results of a research study provides a good exercise in thinking about research.

(d) Answers will vary. The participants should be related to the research question in chapter 2. Sufficient detail should be provided about the participants in regards to gender, SES, ethnicity, and ability. For discussion, explore the links between the participants and the research question. Ask how changing the participants would lead to different outcomes for the study.

Reflection 10.4

There are 4 sources of data in the study: a 10 question pre- and post-test, a 15 question survey, a 7 question interview, and 4 observations of students recorded as journal entries.

Reflection 10.5

The second description is more precise and provides a clearer understanding of the data collection process.

Reflection 10.6

The bulk of the description of the actions describes actions related to teaching. There is also a short description of data collection procedures in the Data Collection section.

Reflection 10.7

1   F
2   R
3   F
4   R

Reflection 10.8

1   A comparison is made between the groups that are on task and those that are off task.
2   Surveys are examined from different perspectives based on the type of question asked and from the perspectives of mean, median, and mode.
3   Findings from a variety of data sources are integrated when interpreting the results.

Reflection 10.9

(a)   Students liked participating in cooperative groups, and there is some evidence their learning was improved. However, improvements are needed in how the groups function. Students achieved some, but not all of the higher level thinking skills during group work. Difficulties may have been caused by lack of familiarity with cooperative learning, language difficulties, the composition of the groups, or a general lack of interest in the activity.

(b)   The strategies for improving this unit can be divided into two major categories: those that use the five principles of cooperative learning to improve group function and those that target higher level thinking. The higher level thinking skills can be further divided into those that are related to scaffolding, those that deal with metacognitive strategies, and those that employ writing to facilitate thinking.

(c)   The strategies described above can be justified through the research literature on cooperative learning, Vygotsky's theories and related research on metacognition, and writing to learn.

Further Reading

Acheson, K.A., & Gall, M.D. (1997). *Techniques in the clinical supervision of teachers: Preservice and inservice applications.* (4th ed.). New York: Longman.

Flanders, N.A. (1970). *Analyzing teacher behavior.* Reading, MA: Addison-Wesley.

Henning, J.E. (2006). Teacher leaders at work: Analyzing standardized achievement data to improve instruction. *Education, 126* (4), 729–737.

Henning, J.E. (2008). *The art of discussion-based teaching: Opening up conversation in the classroom.* New York: Routledge.

Hoover, H.D., Dunbar, S.B., Frisbee, D.A., Oberley, K.R., Bray, G.B., Naylor, R.J., Lewis, J.C., Ordman, V.L., & Qualls, A.L. (2003). *The Iowa tests: Interpretive guide for teachers and counselors.* Ithaca, IL: Riverside Publishing.

Johnson, R.S. (2002). *Using data to close the achievement gap: How to measure equity in our schools.* Thousand Oaks, CA: Corwin Press.

Joyce, B., & Showers, B. (2002). *Student achievement through staff development.* Alexandria, VA: Association for Supervision and Curriculum Development.

Killion, J. (2002). *Assessing impact: Evaluating staff development.* Oxford, OH: National Staff Development Council.

Langer, G.M., Colton, A.B., & Goff, L.S. (2003). *Collaborative analysis of student work: Improving teaching and learning.* Alexandria, VA: Association for Supervision and Curriculum Development.

Little, J.W., Gearhart, M., Curry, M., & Kafka, J. (2003). Looking at student work for teacher learning, teacher community, and school reform. *Phi Delta Kappan, 84* (3), 184–192.

Mercer, N. (1995). *The guided construction of knowledge: Talk amongst teachers and learners.* Clevedon, UK: Multilingual Matters.

Mercer, N. (2000). *Words & minds: How we use language to think together.* NewYork: Routledge.

Nardi, P.M. (2003). *Doing survey research: A guide to quantitative methods.* Boston, MA: Pearson.

Rubin, H.J., & Rubin, I.S. (1995). *Qualitative interviewing: The art of hearing data.* Thousand Oaks, CA: Sage Publications.

Salant, P., & Dillman, D.A. (1994). *How to conduct your own survey.* New York: John Wiley & Sons, Inc.

Streifer, P.A. (2002). *Using data to make better educational decisions.* Lanham, MD: The Scarecrow Press.

References

Bazerman, C. (1988). *Shaping written knowledge*. Madison, WI: University of Wisconsin Press.

Beyer, B.K. (1997). *Improving student thinking: A comprehensive approach*. Boston: Allyn and Bacon.

Bloom, B., Englehart, M., Furst, E., Hill, W., & Krathwohl, D. (1956). *Taxonomy of educational objectives: The classification of educational goals*. Handbook I: *Cognitive domain*. New York: Longmans, Green.

Buckingham, B.R. (1926). *Research for teachers*. New York: Silver Burdett & Co.

Carr, W., & Kemmis, S. (1986). *Becoming critical: Education, knowledge, and action research*. Philadelphia, PA: Falmer Press.

Cochran-Smith, M., & Lytle, S.L. (1993). *Inside/Outside: Teacher research and knowledge*. New York: Teachers College Press.

Cochran-Smith, M., & Lytle, S.L. (1999). Relationships of knowledge and practice: Teacher leaving in communities. *Review of Research in Education 24*, 249–305.

Corey, S. (1949). Curriculum development through action research. *Educational Leadership 7* (3), 147–153.

Corey, S. (1953). *Action research to improve school practices*. New York: Teachers College Press.

Costa, A.L., & Garmston, R.J. (2002). *Cognitive coaching*. Norwood, MA: Christopher-Gordon Publishers.

Dallimore, E.J., Hertenstein, J.H., & Platt, M.B. (2004). Classroom participation and discussion effectiveness: Student-generated strategies. *Communication Education, 53* (1), 103–115.

Dantonio, M., & Beisenherz, P.C. (2001). *Learning to question, questioning to learn: Developing effective teacher questioning practices*. Needham Heights, MA: Allyn and Bacon.

Darling-Hammond, L. (1999). Teacher learning that supports student learning. *Educational Leadership, 55* (5), 6–11.

Designing Surveys and Questionaires. StatPac, Inc. http://www.statpac.com/surveys/index.htm#TOC

Fenstermacher, G. (1994). The knower and the known: The nature of knowledge in the research on teaching. In L. Darling-Hammond, *Review of Research in Education 20* (pp. 3–56). Washington, D.C: American Educational Research Association.

Flanders, N. A. (1970). *Analyzing teacher behavior*. Reading, MA: Addiso-Wesley.

Hobson, D. (2001). Action and reflection: Narrative and journaling in teacher education. In G. Burnaford, J. Fischer, & D. Hobson (Eds.), *Teachers doing research: The power of acting through inquiry* (2nd Edn, pp. 7–27). Mahwah, NJ: Lawrence Erlbaum.

Hoover, H.D., Dunbar, S.B., Frisbee, D.A., Oberley, K.R., Bray, G.B., Naylor, R.J., Lewis, J.C., Ordman, V.L., & Qualls, A.L. (2003). *The Iowa tests: Interpretive guide for teachers and counselors*. Ithaca, IL: Riverside Publishing.

Hubbard, N. (1996). Taking a risk: Learning about physics with young children. In G. Burnaford, J. Fischer, & D. Hobson (Eds.), *Teachers doing research: Practical discussions* (pp. 109–116). Mahwah, NJ: Lawrence Erlbaum.

Hunnicutt, C, W. (1950). Action-research for public schools. *Educational Leadership, 7* (4), 279,284.

Killion, J. (2002). *Assessing impact: Evaluating staff development*. Oxford, OH: National Staff Development Council.

Langer, G.M., Colton, A.B., & Goff, L.S. (2003). *Collaborative analysis of student work: Improving teaching and learning*. Alexandria, VA: Association for Supervision and Curriculum Development.

Little, J.W., Gearhart, M., Curry, M., & Kafka, J. (2003). Looking at student work for teacher learning, teacher community, and school reform. *Phi Delta Kappan, 84* (3), 184–192.

Macintyre, C. (2000). *The art of action research in the classroom*. London: David Fulton Publishers.

McFarland, K.P., & Stansell, J.C. (1993). *Historical perspectives*. In L. Paterson, C.M. Santa, K.G. Short, & K. Smith (Eds.), *Teachers are researchers: Reflection and Action*. Newark, DE: International Reading Association.

McNamara, C. (1999). General guidelines for conducting interviews. St. Paul, MN: The Management Assistance Program for Nonprofits. Available online. http://www.managementhelp.org/evaluatn/intrview.htm#anchor1404957

Mercer, N. (1995). *The guided construction of knowledge: Talk amongst teachers and learners*. Clevedon, UK: Multilingual Matters.

Mercer, N. (2000). *Words & minds: How we use language to think together*. New York: Routledge.

Mills, G.E. (2000). *Action research: A guide for the teacher researcher*: Upper Saddle River, N.J: Merrill.

Noffke, N. (1997). Professional, personal, and practical dimensions of action research. In M. Apple (Ed.), *Review of Research in Education 22*, 305–343.

Patchen, T. (2006). Engendering participation, deliberating dependence: Inner-City adolescents' perceptions of classroom practice. *Teachers College Record, 108* (10), 2053–2079.

Popham, J.W. (2001a). Uses and misuses of standardized tests. *NASSP Bulletin. 85* (6), 24.

Popham, J.W. (2001b). *The truth about testing: An educator's call to action*. Alexandria, VA: Association for Supervision and Curriculum Development.

Qualitative Research Methods: Interviewing. http://uk.geocities.com/balihar_sanghera/qrminterviewing.html

Qualitative Research Methods: Interviewing, University of Florida, College of Liberal Arts and Sciences, http://web.clas.ufl.edu/users/ ardelt/Aging/ QualInt.htm

Rudduck, J. (1988). Changing the world of the classroom by understanding it: A review of some aspects of the work of Lawrence Stenhouse. *Journal of Curriculum and Supervision, 4* (1), 30–42.

Rudduck, J., & Hopkins, D., eds. (1985). *Research as a basis for teaching: Readings from the work of Lawrence Stenhouse*. Portsmouth, NH: Heinemann.

Sadker, D., & Sadker, M. (1985). Is the OK classroom OK? *Phi Delta Kappan, 66* (5), 358–361.

Sauer, R., Popp, M., & Isaacs, M. (1984). Action zone theory and the hearing impaired student in the mainstreamed classroom. *Journal of Classroom Instruction, 19* (2), 21–25.

Schiever, S.W. (1991). *A comprehensive approach to teaching thinking*. Needham Heights, MA: Allyn and Bacon.

Stenhouse, L. (1975). *An introduction to curriculum research and development*. London: Heinemann Educational Books

Van Manen, M. (1990). *Researching lived experience: Human science for an action pedagogy*. Albany, NY: State University of New York Press.

Zeichner, K.M., & Noffke, S.E. (2001). Practitioner research. In V. Richardson (Ed.), *The Handbook for research on teaching*, 4th ed, pp. 298–330. Washington, D.C: American Educational Research Association.

Index